MIRACLE
VICTORY
OVER THE
FLESH-EATING
BACTERIA

David (and Delys) Cowles

GIBBS·SMITH
P
PUBLISHER

Salt Lake City

First Edition
99 98 97 5 4 3 2 1

This is a Peregrine Smith Book, published by
Gibbs Smith, Publisher
P.O. Box 667
Layton, Utah 84041

Designed by Scott Van Kampen
Cover illustration © 1996 by Ron Peterson

Printed and bound in the United States of America

Library of Congress Cataloging-in-Publication Data

Cowles, David L., 1954–
    Miracle victory over the flesh-eating bacteria / by David and
    Delys Cowles. — 1st ed.
            p.   cm.
      ISBN 0-87905-809-9   (pbk.)
      1. Cowles, Davis L., 1954—Health. 2. Necrotizing fasciitis—
    Patients—Utah—Biography.   I. Cowles, Delys, 1957– .
    II. Title.
    RC116.S84C68   1997
    616.9'2—dc21
      [B]   96-39228
                                        CIP

616.92

B2108

MIRACLE VICTORY

OVER THE

FLESH-EATING BACTERIA

David Cowles

Debby Cowles

The Cowles family just before the challenge
of David's disease.

To all those
who have prayed fervently
for someone
they have never met.

Contents

Introduction

This book has been very hard to write. For my part, I have hesitated to add another volume to the pile of existing books describing private spiritual experiences in the most public and, I have often thought, undignified and inappropriate ways.

I have reasons for feeling this way, of course. For one, I spent many years being trained as a skeptic. For eleven years of college I found my assumptions and religious beliefs challenged repeatedly, sometimes by professors or fellow students who wanted to destroy my faith, at other times by those who taught me that, as John Stuart Mill pointed out, even true ideas must be constantly challenged and defended, or they will be little more than prejudices to those who hold them.

My own faith has not come easily. I have had to win it through much struggle and inner conflict. I found the five years I spent earning a Ph.D. at the University of Chicago especially challenging to my faith. While there I specialized in the literature of the English Victorians, who wrote between about 1830 and 1900. The Victorians found themselves confronted on every side by seemingly insurmountable challenges to everything they had grown up believing. Their concerns, doubts, and fears became mine as I studied their lives and works and admired their honesty.

Additionally, persuasive philosophies like deconstruction have helped shape my professional and personal perspectives in important ways and constantly force me to defend my ideas and beliefs.

But in the end, all these studies and struggles have made my faith stronger— as, I believe, it was intended they should. I have long admired Tennyson's description of a friend who struggled for faith:

9

You tell me, doubt is Devil-born.

I know not: one indeed I knew
In many a subtle question versed,
Who touched a jarring lyre at first,
But ever strove to make it true;

Perplexed in faith, but pure in deeds,
At last he beat his music out.
There lives more faith in honest doubt,
Believe me, than in half the creeds.

He fought his doubts and gathered strength,
He would not make his judgment blind,
He faced the specters of the mind
And laid them; thus he came at length

To find a stronger faith his own.

I have long identified with this passage—perhaps presumptuously—and I find in it great wisdom and inspiration.

After all the education, struggles, and doubt, I find I am not always easily persuaded by claims of divine intervention or spiritual insight. Yet, I am thoroughly convinced that the spiritual borders between our lives and God's often become thin, even transparent. I have experienced such manifestations myself, and they have been crucial to my own faith and beliefs.

I do sometimes question, however, the sincerity and wisdom of some people's accounts. I find myself demanding more evidence for assertions and interpretations. Even if someone's vision or revelation really happened just as described, I often suspect it was intended for that person's personal edification rather than for publication or universal application.

This book was difficult to write for more personal reasons as well. In many ways, I am a very private person. There are some things I find I can share readily with students and friends, but others seem too personal for me to talk about easily. Many of the experiences I describe in this book fall into the second, intensely personal category. I have been reluctant to commit some of these to paper. I suppose I feel vulnerable, as if I were standing in front of a class naked. In addition, I still find it somewhat traumatic to remember certain parts of my experience with the "flesh-eating bacteria."

Despite all this, Delys and I have felt a strong compulsion to share our story. We have come to realize that the story is not just ours, or even our family's alone. Many people have contributed at every stage of these events. Doctors, nurses, and therapists performed inspired work and offered constant encouragement and often unforgettable friendship. Friends, colleagues, and neighbors covered my classes, sent me countless letters, cards, and gifts, and gave unselfish (and often anonymous) service. Many reporters and newspeople allowed us to tell the real story instead of focusing on the shock angle of a rare and frightening disease. And thousands of people from many places and religious backgrounds, most of whom had never even met me, offered prayers and hope on my behalf.

This story is as much theirs as ours, and they are entitled to hear it all and to be honored for their contributions to it.

Most important, the influence and evidence of God's hand in all this are too strong even for a part-time skeptic like me to question. We trust and pray that this account will be acceptable praise and thanks to the One who offers life, love, and true learning to us all.

David Cowles
August 1996

Prologue: How I Almost Died the First Time

NOVEMBER 1994

The snow was a foot deep by now, but still the old Suburban clattered its way up the mountain road. Snow crunched beneath the tires, leaving a double line of tracks marking the only passage this high up since the snow had fallen two days ago.

Looking back, I could see how the car had slipped and swerved despite its four-wheel drive. This was my tenth Utah winter since Delys and I accepted teaching jobs with the English Department at Brigham Young University. I had driven in snow many times, but I felt distinctly uneasy now.

"Do you think we should head back down?" I asked.

Dal Sellers, driving comfortably with one hand on the wheel, laughed warmly. "Don't worry. I've pushed cars out of lots worse than this. Besides, I'm pretty sure this road hooks up with the highway about a mile farther on."

Dal looked as if he could pick the car up and put it back on the road if necessary. At 6' 8" and 260 pounds, Dal was the strongest man I had ever known—though I had only met him two days ago.

"Mommy," came a child's voice from the back seat, "I'm thirsty."

Dal's wife, Leslie, turned her head. "I'm sorry, sweetheart, but we'll have to wait until Daddy stops the car. Please stay in your seat." She wasn't any more nervous than her husband.

But I knew Eva was. Eva had lived in Venezuela, Mexico, and now Los Angeles. She had never seen snow falling before. Vernal, Utah, in November was a new experience for her. Tension emanated almost visibly from her in the seat beside me. In the back, six young children were concentrating solely on making as much noise as conceivably possible.

I had met Eva in Caracas, Venezuela, twenty years before while working as a missionary. The Aguilar family and I had unofficially adopted each other, and I had long considered Eva the sister I never had. She had come to Vernal to visit her daughter, Vanessa, who was spending the school year with Dal's family. My son Steven and I had driven Eva to Vernal from the Salt Lake City airport, and I was staying a few days to learn about cattle ranching from Dal for several chapters of my novel-in-progress that are set on a cattle ranch.

The day had started out unusually warm for November. We had left Dal's house wearing light jackets and tennis shoes to look at a house for sale near the bottom of a nearby canyon. No one was really serious about buying the house, but it was fun to look, and the kids desperately needed to get out for a while.

After driving around the property, Dal decided to take us up the canyon so we could appreciate the natural beauty of the area. The snow deepened as the elevation increased. About ten miles up we had stopped for a snowball fight. Red-faced from the cold and wet from the snow, we clambered back into the car. I assumed we would find a place to turn the car around and head back the way we had come. But Dal continued upward. The car's back end fishtailed periodically, and every time it did, my breathing involuntarily stopped. Was Dal crazy, I thought.

Dal had grown up on a remote cattle ranch in Wyoming. He had recently left a ranch he had been working in nearby Colorado after a disagreement with the owner. Dal was temporarily supporting his family by doing freelance mechanic work in Vernal until he could find another situation on a ranch. Dal was a cowboy through and through—not the kind who showed up once a week at Vernal country dances, but the kind who was most comfortable on the back of a horse miles from anywhere or anybody. He was much more at home up here in the hills than back in what only he would call "the big city" of Vernal, population 8,000.

Dal was also the sort of person you didn't make a suggestion to more than once. His cowboy self-confidence was so immense it seemed to overflow his tremendous body, and he was used to charging recklessly into predicaments that would terrify anyone else. To Dal, getting out of dangerous and crazy situations was half the fun of living.

Leslie began describing one of Dal's adventures involving a car stuck in the snow on a lonely back road. I didn't think the tale was particularly well calculated to encourage our confidence just then, but the story was interesting.

Suddenly the Suburban slid to the left. Dal struggled to regain control, but the icy road provided no traction. Slowly, as in a surrealistic dream image, the left

13

rear tire slipped over the road's edge, lurching sideways at a disconcerting angle. The car seemed to bounce once, and the tire nestled securely in a ditch several feet below the level of the road. The Suburban tipped painfully sideways but seemed in no immediate danger of rolling over.

For a moment everyone froze in shocked silence. Then all the kids erupted at once. Eva's right hand still gripped the car's armrest so tightly I thought her hand-prints would be indelibly left in it forever after, and her eyes were open so wide I wondered that her contact lenses didn't fall out. I noticed my own heart beating faster than was comfortable. Dal and Leslie seemed relatively unconcerned.

"Well," Dal said, opening his door with a grin. "It looks like we get to do some pushing."

Everyone nearly fell out of the slanted car, and Dal and I assessed the situation.

"This should be interesting," said Dal. "Normally I'd have blankets, shovels, chains, and a jack in my car. But I just finished fixing this to sell, so it's basically stripped. We'll have to try to push this baby out ourselves."

I looked at the car dubiously. The left rear wheel lay at least three feet below the road level. The front wheel had lodged precariously about halfway between the ditch and the road.

As I approached the rear of the car, I heard a sudden crack. I lurched forward as my right foot unexpectedly dropped into slushy ice and water hidden beneath the snow. I yelled in surprise at the sudden cold and jerked my foot back. As I shifted my weight, my other foot also broke through. I yelled again.

Dal, who had wisely surveyed the scene from a distance, laughed. "Looks like the wheel's in the water, too," he said, more seriously. "This may be a bit tricky."

For over an hour Dal and I pushed and rocked, pled with and threatened the huge Suburban while Leslie worked the gas and steered. In the end we only succeeded in embedding the wheel even deeper, getting snow all over ourselves, and becoming so frustrated that even the normally unflappable Dal was getting into a bad temper.

"This is useless," Dal finally said. Personally, I had come to that conclusion long before—right after the second attempt to push the car out had merely resulted in the wheel spewing snow all over me as it turned furiously without moving the car an inch. But Dal was less easily discouraged, so it took him longer to admit the inevitable.

"Did you say this road connects with the main highway pretty soon?" I asked.

"That's my best guess," Dal said, wiping perspiration from his forehead despite the cold temperature. *"I've never actually driven this far up before."*

"We've only lived here a couple of months," Leslie explained, as if otherwise Dal would have known every inch of the mountains blindfolded. And I suspected he probably would have.

"We'll want to hurry a bit, too," Dal continued, as calmly as if he were merely discussing a shopping trip or a television program. *"Those clouds over in the northwest have been moving toward us pretty steady."*

I hadn't noticed the dark, ominous clouds until Dal pointed them out. And being navigationally handicapped, I frankly couldn't have figured out where northwest was without a compass and an instruction manual. Sense of direction has never been one of my gifts. But I knew enough about Utah winters to be worried.

"That's more snow on the way," I said, trying to keep the concern out of my voice.

"That would be my guess," said Dal with no apparent show of concern.

At first Dal wanted to take off alone, feeling apparently that he had gotten us into this, so he should naturally get us out. I suspected he also felt that I would only slow him down—which was probably true. But Leslie, Eva, and I finally convinced Dal that he and I should go together so that if one of us got hurt, at least there would be someone else there to get help.

"Besides," I argued, *"if you're gone longer than expected, I don't want to have to decide whether to take off after you. Then there might be two of us in trouble instead of one. If we go together, everyone else will know to stay put until we get back."*

We finally all agreed that Dal and I would walk on toward where we hoped we would soon find the highway. We weren't certain what was up ahead, but we were pretty sure we couldn't go back the way we came. We had come at least fifteen miles through steep terrain and deep snow. Dal might have been able to walk all the way back through that (his confidence knew no bounds), but I knew I couldn't.

Once we found the highway, we would hitchhike back to town, buy a set of chains, get a shovel, a jack, and some blankets, buy some food, and return as soon as possible. Leslie and Eva were to keep everyone in the car except for necessary "bathroom" breaks—though I doubted anyone would want to expose body parts to the cold more often than was absolutely necessary—and run the car's heater periodically as needed. We hoped to be back within a couple of hours, before darkness hit at about 5:00.

The next problem was keeping warm while we walked. I had a pretty good winter coat, but Dal, typically, was wearing only a cotton cowboy shirt, the kind with shoulder patches and imitation pearl snaps instead of buttons. Though Dal was nearly twice my weight, the only logical move was for him to wear my coat while I borrowed a lighter one from Eva's daughter, Vanessa. As Dal struggled to get into my coat, the seams stretched, and I expected to hear a rip any second.

Leslie and Eva laughed when we had completed our ritual arming and coat exchange. My coat didn't begin to close around Dal's chest and only came down to about the middle of his stomach. I, on the other hand, had managed to zip up Vanessa's jacket, but it was bright purple and very feminine. We couldn't think of anything to do about our tennis shoes, already wet from sloshing around in the slush trying to get the wheel out of the ditch. And of course we had no gloves or hats.

As Dal and I said good-bye and set out up the hill, I felt an exhilarating sense of adventure. Academic life didn't generally involve physical challenges like this one. Now, I couldn't help imagining myself as some combination of Indiana Jones and Commodore Perry, braving great tribulation to rescue helpless women and children from horrible danger.

The road slanted upward, winding around the side of the mountain. The Suburban soon disappeared behind us as we walked quickly onward. It was just past noon.

Dal estimated that we had come about two miles when we stopped at the road's highest point so far. We looked out over a beautiful expanse of trees and mountains. But there was no highway. We listened for the sound of cars but heard nothing. Before us the road dropped back down the mountain toward the valley below. We couldn't see where it went then, but Dal figured it would go back over the next mountains.

"The highway must be over that ridge instead of this one," he said. "Anyway, if we go far enough, we're bound to hit it eventually."

My misplaced sense of adventure had dissipated gradually over the last mile or so. Now what was left of it vanished. I groaned inwardly. My legs had always been on the weak side, and months of teaching and writing hadn't prepared me for this. To make matters worse, my wet feet were beginning to go numb, Vanessa's jacket was only moderately successful at keeping out the cold, and the temperature suddenly dropped as the sun disappeared behind the edge of the threatening clouds.

Dal started walking without a word. I realized there was nothing to say and followed.

As the road wound downward, the snow depth decreased. The sun still came out from behind the clouds occasionally, making the melting snow sparkle. The leaves cast patterned shadows on the road as we walked. But when clouds blocked the sun, the temperature dropped and everything seemed bleak and silent.

To the inexperienced eye, distances in the mountains seem shorter than they actually are. By the time we reached the top of the next ridge, Dal figured we had come at least four more miles. My legs ached, my gloveless hands shone bright red from the cold, and I couldn't feel my feet at all. The sun was obviously gone for good now.

We could see the road starting down again, but large trees prevented us from seeing very far. We listened for the sound of cars, and Dal thought he could hear something that might be the highway. I desperately hoped it was. I knew I couldn't go much farther like this. I could feel exhaustion setting in, and despite the cold I unzipped Vanessa's coat so the biting air would keep me sharp.

Several miles farther we reached the bottom. What Dal had heard was not a road but an icy stream. At this lower elevation there was less snow, and we could see occasional patches of grassy meadows. We were grateful for moments when little or no snow covered parts of the road.

Near the stream at the valley's lowest point, our asphalt road ended as it ran into another road made only of red dirt. Exhausted, we sat to rest on some conveniently placed boulders and discussed the situation. There was no point in going back: we would be no better off, and I, at least, could never make it. Dal could see that I was on the verge of collapse, and even he showed signs of fatigue.

Dal and I agreed that our only hope was to follow the new road downhill. I didn't really want to go uphill again anyway, and, as Dal succinctly put it, "Town is down."

"We'd better get started before my legs cramp up," I said, standing.

Another mile or so farther, the road headed steeply uphill again. I was beginning to feel desperate. My legs plodded along in pain, though my hands and feet felt nothing. I concentrated on each step as if it would be the last I would have to take. I was beginning to get lightheaded, and I staggered more and more often. I took my coat off completely, hoping the cold would keep me conscious.

Sensing my desperate situation, Dal kept me talking—about books, children, politics, anything to keep me going. I recognized what he was doing, but I appreciated it and played along.

Somehow we kept moving for several more miles until the road, deep in snow, *again started winding downward. By now the sun, hidden by heavy cloud cover, was low on the horizon. Snow had begun to fall lightly.*

We worried about those back in the Suburban, partly, I suspect, to call our attention away from the seriousness of our own situation. Once night fell, we would be nearly helpless. The temperature would plummet, we would be all but blind without moon or starlight, and we would quickly freeze to death. Since we had left the car, we had seen no tire prints to indicate that anyone else had passed this way.

Amazingly, I managed to keep walking. Another mile passed. I knew I could not continue much farther, and I wondered what Dal would do when I finally collapsed. I was pretty sure he would try to carry me. If he left me in the snow, I would certainly freeze to death very quickly. But I knew that even Dal couldn't go on much farther with the extra burden.

I had silently prayed for help many times on our journey, but now my prayer was desperate and rose from the depths of my soul. "Lord, I think I have about three more steps left in me." That was no exaggeration. My frozen, exhausted legs simply would not go on. "Lord, we need your help. This would be a really good time for you to send somebody to help us." I had too little energy to say anything else.

"Dal," I managed to say, "I think I've reached the end."

Even as I said that, I heard a sound that seemed completely foreign to that remote and silent place. It was the whine of an engine. A moment later a red-and-white Chevy pickup came fishtailing around the bend below us. Dal waved and ran down the hill toward it. I walked—slowly—with a last remnant of energy I didn't know I had. That's how God works, I thought. He makes you push yourself until you can't possibly do any more, and then—maybe—he sends help.

In the truck were three teenage boys. They had come up here joyriding after school with a snowmobile tied up in the pickup's cargo bed. They didn't even have four-wheel drive. How they made it up that far through the deepening snow remains a mystery to me.

Dal convinced the young men that they didn't want to go any farther up that road or they would meet the same fate the Suburban had. They reluctantly decided he was right, and Dal offered to pay for their gas if they would take us back to town. We climbed into the cargo bed and positioned ourselves as comfortably as possible on either side of the snowmobile.

The driver had to back the car down the road for over a mile before he found a place he could turn around. My mind and body wanted more than anything to sleep, but I had to stay awake to keep from being thrown out of the truck on the bumpy road.

We drove on and on, until I was amazed at how far we had to go. And we drove still farther. The driver, who had been watching the odometer, told us it was just over twenty miles from where he had picked us up until we reached the first house. The only tire tracks we saw until just before that house were those the pickup had made on the way up.

By the time we got back to the Suburban with tools, blankets, and a bucket of chicken, it was after 9:00. I was just beginning to sense feeling in my toes, positioned strategically under the heating vent of Dal's old blue pickup. Dal and I took the short route, following the Suburban's tracks back up the canyon. We saw snowmobile tracks that went to within half a mile of the stranded car before turning around, but no evidence of any other vehicles. With no food, nothing to drink, and not even a scrap of paper to keep them entertained, Leslie and Eva had managed to keep the nine children calm and safe, despite their own deepening concerns. Eva told me that they didn't begin to worry until it started snowing hard and darkness fell.

Even with chains, two jacks, and the pickup, it took Dal and me more than an hour to free the Suburban. I drove the Suburban back to Vernal while Dal drove the pickup we had come in. The chains barely kept the car from sliding off the road again in the deepening snow. By the time we reached Dal and Leslie's house in Vernal, it was nearly midnight.

Had those boys in the pickup not come just when they did, Dal and I both would have died, and our family members would have been stranded far from help without food. I have no doubt that the pickup appeared as a direct answer to my desperate prayer. I knew I should have been dead, and as I thanked the Lord, I felt a deep spiritual conviction that for reasons of his own, God had preserved our lives. It plainly was not my time to go.

Less than a month later I would have occasion to discover that again, and in a big way.

It's Just the Flu

At Christmastime we were all worn out. Most English professors are. Between David and me, we had taught five courses and more than two hundred students in BYU's English Department that fall semester. Finally, at three in the afternoon on December 22, 1994, we were ready with grades finished and family packed.

The black duffel-bag suitcases we bought when we directed the university's London Study Abroad program bulged with clothes, toys, and the inevitable books. Two years ago we looked like the Family Von Trapp in their traveling clothes trudging in the snow off to Switzerland. This year we looked like a family with warm California in its eyes. This year we were going to rest for a week at my parents' home near Los Angeles.

David nicked his finger zipping up his bag, but it didn't bleed, so he ignored it. When I called my parents to tell them we would arrive late, my father, Merwin Waite, quietly told me his ninety-four-year-old mother had just died, which meant we would be in California for her funeral. After a quick stop at BYU to turn in grades, we were off, driving south on I-15. But the relaxing vacation in Hacienda Heights never really evolved.

We stopped in Beaver, Utah, and Las Vegas, Nevada, to grab food, use the bathrooms, and fill up the car with gas. By the time we reached California, everyone was asleep, and I didn't want to wake them up, so I pulled over occasionally, left the car running, and stretched my back on the side of the road. By the end I was forcing myself to stay awake to finish the drive. We arrived safely, although it was about 2:00 A.M. and my parents were a bit worried. But I knew we could recover from the long twelve-hour trip and make up for lost sleep during our leisurely days at my parents' home.

The day before Christmas, David noticed his finger was slightly infected and asked for antiseptic and a bandage. That night he noticed some pain under his arm. We stayed up late on Christmas Eve wrapping presents, assembling toys, and making sure we had an even distribution of gifts. The next day was Christmas, and the children woke us up at the agreed hour of 8:00 A.M. For some reason, they would never give in to our requests for "just fifteen minutes more sleep, please." We dragged ourselves out of bed, threw on our robes, and lined everyone up at the door, youngest to oldest. Then we all ran in and looked for our names on presents. David sat on the couch, and after a half hour, he asked my mother for something to eat—maybe a banana—because he felt a bit weak.

As the last child opened the last gift, David suddenly began to shake with chills as he slowly tipped over on the couch. "I think that banana didn't sit well," he understated. I could see he was coming down with something, probably the intestinal flu, so I volunteered to stay home with him while all of the others went to church that morning. Maybe this is just a twenty-four-hour bug, I silently thought as he tried to nap. I knew that David could get extremely sick when he got the flu, so I hoped this one would be mild. As soon as my parents and our children left for church, David threw up in the bathroom, so we set a bucket on some newspaper on the bedroom floor. David tried to sleep some more, but found himself in the bathroom with diarrhea. By now his arm was really aching, and by the end of the day he was walking around holding his right side, too. Strangely enough, he had no fever, but he couldn't eat or drink anything without losing it.

The next day was Monday, December 26, a holiday for most people. By afternoon I knew this wasn't the twenty-four-hour variety of intestinal flu, so I hoped it was only a thirty-six-hour kind, if there was such a thing. David's discomfort was increasing, but he couldn't keep down any ibuprofen to help relieve the excruciating pain. I called our doctor in Provo, but the only person we could get was an assistant to our doctor's partner. "Be more concerned when he has a fever," was the general gist.

By now the pain was so intense that David would do whatever he could to distract himself. He would wander around the house and sometimes sit and watch television, but I would shoo him back into the bedroom so he wouldn't infect anyone else. My brother Clint and my sister, Wendy, and her family

21

had arrived from Colorado and Arizona for Grandma's funeral. I didn't want anyone else catching this awful flu, so I tried to isolate David. My parents dug up a small portable black-and-white television for David to watch. The picture was hopelessly fuzzy, and the channel selection was small, but the sound gave him a way to direct his attention away from the pain.

In the meantime, I was assigned to speak at my Grandma Waite's funeral, since I am the oldest granddaughter. I kept notes for several days about what I wanted to say. I stayed up late Monday night writing my talk for the funeral the next day.

Tuesday morning David looked green. He staggered around the house like a walking corpse. By this time he could hardly stand the pain of his arm and his side, so he took baths to distract himself, which drove me crazy because I was trying to get five children ready for the funeral service and he always had the bathroom tied up. No one knew what to do to help David because he would just walk slowly down the hall moaning and then walk back to the bed and lie down. My brother Clint was going to fly home to Denver right after the funeral. I noticed he stayed far away from David and hung out at the neighbors' house so he wouldn't catch what David had.

Since David was no better and hadn't eaten anything for two days, I agreed to try the doctor one more time. I called his office in Provo. This time I actually got to speak with the doctor, and he told me David's symptoms sounded a lot like the flu that was going around Utah. I told him David's aches were extremely painful. He said we could take him to a doctor in California, but we would get the same advice.

I asked my father and my brother to give a healing blessing to David. Because we thought this was a bad flu and had no idea what was coming, we were surprised when my father said, "I bless you that the thing that is eating you will be purged, and that through this experience you will gain more compassion and understanding for people and what they suffer." My sister, brother, and I all remember these words very clearly, and my sister recorded them in her journal that night.

I decided that we could probably leave David alone for an hour and a half while we all attended Grandma's funeral. Then I would come right home and take him to a doctor. I knew he was in horrible pain, but he was walking around all right, and he was basically taking care of himself, so I wasn't too worried. I figured he would be in agony whether I was there or at the funeral, so we left him alone and all piled in the van to drive to the church a mile away.

Grandma Waite had lived a long, full ninety-four years, so her funeral was a mix of grief and joy. Grandma had five sons and no daughters, so when I came along as the first granddaughter (after six grandsons), she was thrilled. I stood at the pulpit and told stories about Waite women being strong. I talked about Grandma living through the Great Depression, and how this had affected her whole life. I talked about her faith and her religious strength, about her work ethic and efforts not to let anyone get too big-headed. I talked about the lessons we had learned from her determination and struggles.

Then the world turned surrealistic. As I sat down, my neighbor ran a note up to me: "Your husband has been taken to the hospital by ambulance." My next thought was that David was probably dehydrated and had overreacted in a very dramatic (and very expensive) way by calling an ambulance. I stayed for a few minutes to sing the alto part in a song with my female cousins. Then I gave the note to my father, asked my mother to watch the children, and took off to their house. At home I found Roxanne Bryant, our neighbors' daughter-in-law. She was late leaving for the funeral, so she had been at home when the ambulance arrived. She told me David had been taken to a hospital in Whittier, but she didn't know what was wrong with him. I called and found he was at Whittier Medical Center. "Is my husband okay?" I asked. They answered, "Yes." I drove quickly to the hospital, thinking David was probably doing fine. Instead, I found my husband on the edge of death.

· · ·

Tuesday morning I felt sicker than I had ever been before. The body aches that accompanied this "flu" had become so painful, I could hardly stand to sit or lie down or do anything. I kept taking hot baths, hoping for no good reason that this would reduce the pain somewhat. It never did, but at least filling up the bathtub helped distract me.

When everyone left for the funeral, the house was strangely quiet. Eleven kids and seven adults can make a lot of noise. In the silence I prayed for the strength to endure this horrible sickness. And I hinted that if God found it convenient, he might consider making the pain end soon.

Suddenly I sensed clearly within my mind these words: "You need an ambulance. Now." It wasn't an actual voice, but it was so insistent and forceful that I could not ignore it. Still, I hesitated. I'm not the sort of person who calls 911 for myself. If one of my children were in danger, I would call in an instant. But whether because of latent male machismo or just being too cheap to pay for an ambulance, I am the kind of person who would die sitting next to the telephone wondering whether I was really sick enough to call for help.

Again the almost audible voice said, "You need an ambulance. Now!" I had had enough experience with that voice to obey it this time. I limped my way to the phone and dialed 911.

When a woman's voice answered, I repeated the words I had heard in my mind: "I need an ambulance. Now." The woman confirmed my address and promised to send paramedics. Then she tried valiantly to keep me on the line and conscious. "Sit up straight and keep talking," she said. "Put both feet on the floor." I did my best, but my body was becoming increasingly uncooperative. Finally I just couldn't do what she asked any longer. "I'm going to hang up now," I said, as politely as I could. As I reached to hang up the phone, I could hear her frantically trying to keep me on the line, but I was past caring.

I walked to the bedroom with excruciating slowness, leaning against the wall for support. With great effort I managed to exchange my robe for sweatpants and a T-shirt. Sensing that I was losing consciousness, I stumbled to unlock the front door, then literally crawled to the living-room couch, collapsing in dizziness and pain.

A few minutes later two fire trucks and an ambulance pulled up outside the house, lights flashing wildly. A whole army of uniformed paramedics jumped out. Someone pounded on the door and called, "Paramedics."

"Come in," I called out, as loudly as I could. Apparently that wasn't very loud, because the knocking continued. Finally someone opened the door.

"I'm over here," I moaned.

Immediately I was surrounded by people prodding, poking, and questioning me. While I tried to answer, one looked up from my left arm and said, "I can't get any blood pressure at all. Try the other arm." That one was equally unsuccessful. "Let's take him in," someone finally said. The paramedics strapped me to a gurney and hauled me out to the ambulance. Just before they put me in, Roxanne Bryant rushed out of the house next door to see what was wrong. "Tell Delys," was all I could manage to say.

During the ride to the hospital, I first heard the set of questions that medical personnel would ask Delys and me over and over again.

"Are you a heavy smoker?"

"No, I don't smoke."

"Have you been drinking excessive amounts of alcohol recently?"

"No, I don't drink."

They would pause as if surprised, then ask suspiciously, "Are you sure?"

Finally I said, "Of course I'm sure. I may be in pain, but I'm not stupid." Even that didn't seem to satisfy them, but at least they quit asking for a while.

The next thing I remember is finding myself on a curtained-off cot in Emergency. An Asian man I would come to know as Dr. Shin was asking me the same questions everyone else had while monitoring my vital signs. He was obviously concerned about my condition but uncertain what my problem was. "You may find this uncomfortable, but we have to insert a tube through your nose." I started to say, "What—," but Dr. Shin had already begun worming the plastic tube into my left nostril. I gagged as it painfully passed through my nose and down my throat. After a few minutes I grew relatively accustomed to the tube, though I found it perpetually uncomfortable.

Whenever Dr. Shin came back, I asked him if he could remove the nose hose and perhaps give me something to reduce the pain. Each time, he explained patiently that he could do neither until they figured out what was wrong with me and managed to get my blood pressure and other vital signs up.

I heard Dr. Shin and another physician as they discussed my symptoms while waiting for an X-ray machine to arrive. Apparently I showed signs of heart attack, but some of my symptoms were inconsistent with that diagnosis.

After what seemed like just longer than forever, Dr. Shin told me that the X-rays had revealed what looked like a kidney stone but showed no conclusive cause for my condition. He thought surgery would be necessary, and soon, whatever the cause.

"Could you remove the kidney stone while you're in there?" I asked. I had heard that kidney stones could be very painful.

Dr. Shin smiled. "We'll worry about that problem later. Let's fix the one causing you all this trouble first."

Finally another doctor came in and told me he wanted to take an MRI. I had no idea what that was, but I was in no position to argue. I was wheeled to another room, where my torso was exposed. Technicians moved me to a kind of tray that allowed my body to enter the unit. The MRI took about an hour.

As the technicians slid me out, someone noticed that a blackish-purple spot about four inches in diameter had formed on my side. It had not been there when I entered the machine.

"Have you been kicked in that side?" someone asked me. No one had told me about the spot, so the question seemed absurd.

"No," I said. "Why would anyone do that?"

"Maybe you were drunk and didn't notice," someone else suggested.

Here we go again, I thought.

I could see the physician speaking to Delys with considerable animation but too softly for me to hear. Why don't they talk to me, I wondered. I guess I'll have to wait for Delys to tell me what the doctor said.

That was my last fully conscious thought for six days.

Like a Shark Bit Him

When I arrived at the hospital I walked in the back way to the emergency room because I didn't know where it was. Actually this was best because I was able to walk right up to David's bed and talk with the nurses and doctors instead of being delayed in the waiting room. I discovered that my husband had almost no blood pressure, and that he had IVs full of dopamine to increase it. Dopamine is a drug that pulls blood in from the body's extremities to the heart and other vital organs. David's kidneys and other organs had mysteriously shut down. He had a tube going up his nose that I later learned was vacuuming out his stomach.

"Hi, honey," I smiled as I walked in.

"Hi," he said in the tone of "look what is happening to me."

I could tell this wasn't dehydration.

A technician announced, "We are going to use the X-ray machine in this next curtained room, so all visitors out." I obliged and stood out by the nurses' work counter. A doctor asked me if my husband was a heavy smoker.

"No, he has never smoked."

"Has he been drinking alcohol heavily?"

"No, he doesn't drink alcohol."

"Is he diabetic?"

"No."

"Was he drunk last night?"

"No, he doesn't drink. He is normally healthy, and he eats a low-cholesterol diet. He even exercises regularly."

The X-ray technicians were finished with the man who was moaning from a heart attack in the next partitioned-off room. As I saw David again, he mentioned what excruciating pain he was in. He could hardly stand the muscle aches that had been going on for several days. "Please could they give me something for the pain?" I checked with the nurses, and they said they could give him nothing until his blood pressure rose.

Another doctor came and told us he was a heart specialist called in to operate on David because they thought he was having a heart attack. The tests, though, showed that his heart was fine, and the doctors ruled out heart attack. David reminded me that his EKG six months earlier had been so perfect that the doctor had checked the equipment to make sure it was working correctly. Now they were stumped. His body was in shock and shutting down, and no one had any idea why.

"Was he drunk last night?"

"Absolutely not," I replied for the third time that day. "He does not drink alcohol."

"Well, we will take him to ultrasound and then maybe do an MRI."

I had a few moments to talk to David and hold his hand. He told me about his strong impression to call for an ambulance and how the paramedics had not been able to find a pulse. He also said he had never been in greater pain than he was at that moment because so much of his arm and side ached. He could hardly stand it.

The technicians took him to the ultrasound testing, and I went into the emergency waiting room. These rooms are generally noisy and stressful, and this one was no exception. Small bored children were crying, and the ubiquitous talk show was playing on the television. I gave the receptionist all of David's insurance information and sat down and waited. I can't think when the television is blaring, so I read a magazine article about organizing closets. The nurses said they would come out to get me when David returned from the ultrasound, but it took longer than I expected, and the receptionist tired of me asking. So I read about make-overs and buying career clothes on a budget, fixing quick meals in under thirty minutes, and talking to your teenagers. Still he wasn't back.

An hour and three magazines later, the receptionist called my name, and I went back to David's room to discover that they still could find no cause for his symptoms. This time they were going to try an MRI, and so I followed them and waited in the MRI waiting room trying to figure out what MRI stood for.

They said it would be about an hour and it stood for Magnetic Resonance Imaging.

After half an hour, I saw my mother walking down the hall, and I called to her. She had been at the hospital for almost forty-five minutes looking for us. My mother had stayed at the funeral and helped with my children. After the services, my parents and children drove to the cemetery for the grave-side service, and then back to the church where the women's organization of our church had prepared dinner for all the family members. Before eating, my mother slipped away and went home to find out what had happened to David. Roxanne Bryant told Mom that when I originally called the hospital, the nurse had told me David was okay, and that I had suspected he was just dehydrated. When Mom called, though, the hospital personnel would only say that he was in critical condition. As soon as she found me, we both sat down and I told her all about David's condition. After that we waited some more, this time without magazines.

Eventually the doctors came to talk to me. They immediately asked how David got that big purple bruise on his side.

"I don't know, I've never seen a big bruise on him. It wasn't there before."

"Was he drunk in an alley last night and someone kicked him?"

Here we go again, I thought.

"You know, he really doesn't drink alcohol. He wasn't drunk in some alley last night, he was sick in bed. We're very religious people. We don't drink, and we don't smoke. I promise you he was not drunk last night." I couldn't seem to convince them.

Then the doctors conferred for a while and examined David some more. "Are you sure that bruise wasn't there before?"

"I would have noticed," I replied.

"We think we know what it is, then," they said as they stepped out into the hall away from David's hearing. The doctors told me they were afraid he had necrotizing fasciitis, which is popularly known as "the flesh-eating bacteria."

"You've heard of this flesh-eating bacteria in the press lately, haven't you?"

I vaguely remember standing in line at the grocery store and seeing headlines in the weekly tabloids mentioning something to that effect. But I believed the headlines about flesh-eating bacteria about as much as I believed that Elvis was a space alien with a new diet plan.

Then they told me about the president of the university at Northridge who contracted this disease and died a few days later. This had happened only a few months previously, so the story was still fresh in many local people's minds.

It seemed almost too strange to be true. Here we were, hundreds of miles from home, on vacation, enjoying Christmas, attending Grandma's funeral, and wham, my husband was sick, barely alive, and the doctors had diagnosed a tabloid-type disease. I wondered if people were going to dub this the "professor" disease or something silly like that.

By this time my mother was by my side. After she heard the diagnosis, she said, "Oh come on, there is no way he has a disease like that."

"This is an extremely aggressive bacteria and can spread as fast as an inch an hour. The bacteria and their toxins destroy the skin and soft tissue and shut down vital organs. Our only recourse is to take him into surgery right away and try to cut out the infected parts. I am going to open him up from wrist to hip, and he may end up looking like a shark bit him. Even so, this disease is so fast moving, he only has a 5- to 10-percent chance of living through the night."

I let this sink in. I knew that if he had a 5- to 10-percent chance of living, he had a 90- to 95-percent chance of dying. This seemed like a kind way of telling me my husband was probably going to die, and that he would probably die tonight. But I also knew that he still had a chance, and I knew how to increase the odds. The doctors several times came to tell me how serious David's condition was and how little chance he had of living. But I am a fairly strong person, especially in a crisis. My calm confused them, and they asked if I understood the gravity of the situation.

I answered, "I do realize how serious this is, but I say a 5- to 10-percent chance is worth going for. Let's go for life. Let's save him."

"Okay, we will operate as soon as we can get everything ready." The doctor told me this kind of surgery wasn't really his area of specialty, but Dr. Shin had left, and we needed to act now.

The nurse pulled my mother and me aside. "You know your husband doesn't have much chance. If I were you I would bring the children in to see him one last time." She told me about her own father dying suddenly when she was young, and how she regretted that she didn't get to say good-bye to him. She didn't want this to happen to our children.

My mother rushed home to Hacienda Heights, about fifteen minutes away. On the way she ran into construction and detours. Frustrated, she arrived home thirty minutes later. "I need all of the Cowles children with your shoes on and in the car right now. Hurry." The children knew their father was in the hospital, but they had no idea how sick he was. Mom told them a little bit about the disease on the way back to the hospital.

Meanwhile, David was not quite as coherent as before. His body had stabilized somewhat, and he was on morphine.

"Did you know you have a bruise on your side?" I asked.

"No."

"They are going to operate on you in a little while and find out what is wrong with you."

"I think it's kidney stones or something," David replied. I let him continue to think it.

"Mom is bringing the children so they can wish you well in your operation." I secretly prayed that they would arrive before the surgeons took David away.

"Oh, she doesn't need to go to that trouble." He had no idea that he was near death, and I thought he would go into shock again if I told him outright, so I just talked about the operation in a general sense. By now David had IVs and tubes and sensors all over his body. The room was full of blinking lights, monitors, and beep-beep beep-beep sounds. I let him rest awhile.

My father arrived with my brother-in-law, Bob Jensen, and they gave him another healing blessing before the operation. Dad sat on a hard chair in the hall afterward; his face looked worried and starkly white. He realized that his oldest daughter, at the rather young age of thirty-seven, was likely to be a widow with five children and overwhelming responsibilities. And besides, he had always hated the sight of needles and IVs.

When the children arrived, they were in shock. They had spent the morning at a funeral, the first for most of them. Then they came home to find that their usually healthy father might die. Emotions ran high. The nurse prepared them to see their father covered with tubes, and we went in to talk to him. We wished him well, squeezed his hand, then gathered out in the hall, where the nurse brought us apple juice and chairs so we

31

wouldn't faint. Robby (12) was pale with shock, so he put his head between his knees.

I went back in to be with David alone. I knew this might be the last time I spoke to him, so I bent down close to his face and talked to him from my heart. "David, I want you to choose life. Choose life, David."

As the orderlies rolled David into surgery, my family moved to the surgery waiting room. We were all alone, so we knelt together in a circle, and each of us offered a prayer for David's life. I started: "Heavenly Father, medical science does not know what is wrong with David. But you know. The doctors are not sure how to treat his sickness. But you know. Please bless the doctors that they will know how to help David. Please bless David that his body will fight off this disease so that he can live. Please hear our prayers and let David live. But we know that your will is best. And please bless us that we will be able to cope with whatever your will is."

Nancy, a concerned nurse, found crayons and paper for our two youngest, Steven and Marissa, and made arrangements so I could make long-distance phone calls. My oldest daughter, Cristie, and I went into an unused office to phone friends. I called Leon and Beth Cowles, David's parents, in Portland, Oregon. The news was sobering, and they decided to fly out the next day if they could get tickets. I called Beth Hedengren, my good friend, neighbor, and colleague in the English Department.

"Delys, are you back already?" she cheerfully greeted me.

"No, Beth, I have something very serious to tell you. I am in California calling from a hospital phone. David seems to have necrotizing fasciitis, a flesh-eating bacteria. He has been given a 5- to 10-percent chance of living through the night. Right now he is in surgery, and the next two hours will probably decide whether or not he lives. But I believe in miracles and the power of faith and prayer. Will you call everyone we know and ask them to pray for David?"

My conversation with Bruce Bryan, the head of our local church congregation, was similar.

Within an hour nearly the entire English Department, our congregation, other friends, and our extended family were actively praying for David. And David's parents gallantly worked to find plane tickets from Portland to Los Angeles, unfortunately the same week as the Rose Bowl (the Oregon Ducks were playing for the first time in years). There were no tickets available—at any price.

The nurse, Nancy, poked her head into the waiting room. "I know you are very religious people. Are you vegetarians?"

"No, we aren't vegetarians."

"Okay, I am going off shift now, and I am going to bring you all back some food." She returned later with bags of McDonald's fries and hamburgers and drinks—lots of food for a drained family. She wouldn't let us pay her back. I ate for the first time since early that morning, but I hardly tasted the food.

Dr. Grim and the Darkest Hour

The scary thing about waiting for surgery results is that you don't know which emotion to prepare for. I remember lying on the floor because I felt weak. Any minute someone could walk in and tell me my husband had died, or that he didn't really have this disease and would be fine.

When the surgeons finally came, they had encouraging news. Dr. Shin had arrived back at the hospital just in time to perform the surgery. The disease had not progressed as far as they had expected, so they did not have to cut out much soft tissue—yet. We all cheered and felt that the Lord had answered our prayers. The surgeons said that as they cut open David's side, fluids poured out of his body and soaked Dr. Shin's pants and socks. The surgeons wondered whether they should begin taking antibiotics to prevent themselves from contracting the disease. They decided they were not in danger, but Dr. Shin had to throw away his contaminated clothes.

David was now open from his right wrist, up his arm, down his side to his hip. They just wrapped him in gauze afterward.

Several friends from my parents' church came to the hospital to find out how things were going. They got in by telling the staff they were our brothers and sisters. In a large sense, I suppose they are. Mickey Bladh and her husband, Eric, brought me a hospital survival bag that had fruit and snacks. I carried the bag around with me for a few days. When the commotion quieted, my father took our children home to sleep. Wendy and Bob and their children left my parents' home for Arizona around midnight so they wouldn't be in the way.

The surgeons told us they wanted to move David to another hospital four miles away when he stabilized. About midnight an ambulance arrived to take David, but his blood pressure was too low for them to move him. He was semiconscious after the surgery, so I went in and talked to him. I held his hand and talked about simple things such as the colors in the room and how proud I was of him. His blood pressure rose, and the ambulance took him away. My mother and I followed.

It was now midnight, and although it seemed like a week, it had only been around twelve hours since David dialed 911. The new hospital was Presbyterian Intercommunity in Whittier. After getting David admitted, I found him in the Critical Care Unit (CCU). Now he was assigned one full-time Critical Care nurse, and the intensity of care rose remarkably. At the new hospital, the doctors (David had a team of about twelve different doctors) told me they were going to attack this bacteria on three fronts: first, antibiotic therapy, which would require a few days to take effect; next, surgery, cutting out all necrotized (dead) and infected tissue; and third, a hyperbaric chamber. That night around 2:00 A.M., they called in their respiratory technicians and put David in the hyperbaric chamber for the first time.

. . .

Despite the considerable time I spent in the hyperbaric chamber, I retain few memories of anything associated with it. Most of what I do remember is not pleasant.

The hyperbaric chamber, better known for its use on underwater divers with the "bends," looks like a tiny, two-person submarine. It is basically a long cylinder of reinforced steel with windows like portholes. One end opens to admit a patient and a respiratory therapist. I have little recollection about the outside of the hyperbaric chamber, though I vividly remember being slid into it on several occasions.

Once the patient and doctor are inside, the end is tightly sealed, the atmospheric pressure is increased, and pure oxygen is pumped in. This high-pressure, oxygen-rich atmosphere forces oxygen into the body's cells and allows healing to occur at a much faster rate than in normal air pressure. The hospital's medical staff felt strongly that daily regimens of hyperbaric oxygen were essential to my survival.

It turned out that I was again blessed in getting sick where I did. There were only three hyperbaric chambers in the Los Angeles area, and I managed to contract necrotizing fasciitis just a few miles from one of them. People sometimes ask me if I resented getting sick so far from home. I generally explain that had all this happened back in Provo, where I would not have had access to a hyperbaric chamber, I would almost certainly have died.

The doctors and assistants who worked with the hyperbaric chamber also saw their task as crucial to my survival. Their perspective was very different from that of my family and friends. They weren't praying for miracles; they were carefully sterilizing their equipment before each treatment and working out the details of my care. One staff member explained to me later, "We felt that if we did everything perfectly, kept everything absolutely sterile, and made no mistakes anywhere, you might have a small chance of surviving this thing." The hyperbaric staff sometimes had to come to the hospital in the middle of the night to give me emergency treatments.

Despite the hyperbaric chamber's crucial benefits in my treatment, once I became conscious enough to have some sense of what was going on, I hated the thing.

To begin with, the process of getting me into the chamber was fairly involved. After wheeling me down several hallways to the hyperbaric room, orderlies would have to lift me carefully from my gurney to the chamber's sliding table. Actually getting me into the chamber proved extremely difficult because I came with so many attachments: my large and ever-changing collection of IVs, monitors, tubes, wires, and whatnot. Some of these could be connected through the chamber's walls to tubes and wires inside, but others had to go in with me. Staff members had to slide me in slowly and very carefully to keep from pulling something loose.

Once inside, with the therapist sitting behind me, I just lay there for two hours while the pressure and oxygen levels climbed slowly, maintained for a while, then came slowly down. After the treatment, I would emerge from the chamber shining lobster red.

. . .

By now David looked terrible. He was so swollen, the staff thought he weighed more than 200 pounds, but I knew he only weighed about 150. Fortunately, we had taken off his wedding ring before the first surgery, and I wore it for several days next to my own. David had a tube going down his throat, one down his nose, one into a central catheter in his chest for all the IVs, and another into his arm for blood samples. He had electrodes all over his body and a clamp on his finger to monitor oxygen in his blood. His right arm and his torso were wrapped in bandages. The only place I could touch him was his left hand, so I held it a lot. Every time the doctors sliced his body, they left the wounds open and just wrapped them with gauze. There was no reason to stitch him up, since they were going to operate again the next day. Besides, there was increasingly less skin to stitch anything to.

"Continue to give him fluids," ordered his Critical Care doctor, Dr. Saketkhoo. "It's impossible to give him too much. His body is like a sieve—everything seeps out the open incisions."

David couldn't talk because of the tube down his mouth, but he could blink and squeeze my hand. One time when he was semiconscious, I spoke to him.

"Do you want to know where you are?"

"Yes, desperately," his eyes told me.

"We are in a hospital in Whittier. Do you want to know what is wrong with you?" He looked quite confused. He nodded as vigorously as he could, which wasn't much.

"You have an aggressive bacterial infection. You are very sick. I called your parents and told them, and they are flying down here to see you."

David looked puzzled, as if saying, "Why are my parents coming? Tell them not to go to all this trouble." I wanted David to fight for life and not give up, but I thought that if he knew he was on the brink of dying, he would be shocked. Consequently, I tried to make all the visits from children, parents-in-law, and parents look like a normal thing concerned people do, not like a final good-bye march.

. . .

My memories of the next six days are vivid but detached and retain a certain surrealistic, fuzzy quality. I underwent major, lifesaving surgery six times in those six days, so I constantly suffered from the effects of anaesthesia. When that wore off, I was on high doses of morphine.

All my memories seem to be at night, though I believe this was because my room was always darkened. Outside, the busy desk for that section of the hospital made me believe I was in a back room at some sort of business establishment, perhaps a mail-order retailer. I remember people bringing mail and making other deliveries, but I never managed to connect what people said with any general sense of where I was or what was happening to me. I recall wondering—with the paranoia that sometimes accompanies morphine—whether I had been kidnapped. Perhaps I was being held here, drugged out of my mind, for some mysterious purpose. I learned much later that the hospital staff had tied my hands down so I wouldn't pull the tubes out. *Perhaps this contributed to my sense of captivity. As nearly as I can recall, it never occurred to me that I was in a hospital.*

I do retain several vivid memories from this period. I remember a doctor and nurse trying to adjust my bed, and having difficulties with a mechanism that I later learned kept squeezing and releasing my legs to keep the blood flowing through them. I remember Delys bringing my oldest children to see me. That memory, still rather vague, features Delys bending over me and repeating "Choose life, David. Choose life." I don't think I had the slightest idea what she was talking about. Her appearance somehow reminded me of a Fizzies commercial I hadn't thought of since I was a child, though now I have no idea what the connection might have been.

I also remember someone asking me if I knew where I was. I tried to answer but could not because of the tube down my throat. I shook my head. "You're in a special medical facility," she said. "You've been moved here because you are very, very sick, and we have the facilities to take care of you." Sick, I thought. Imagine that. Then I lapsed back into unconsciousness.

. . .

I sat in a chair next to my husband's bed. My head kept nodding and my chin kept hitting my chest whenever I dozed off. It was 3:00 A.M. or so, and I had not slept a full eight hours in a long time. But I didn't want to go home to sleep because I would have to leave David. The head nurse pulled me aside and said I could rest a little in the staff bed on that floor, so I followed her down a dark hall and into a little room that had a bed, a mirror, a chair, and a bathroom. "You can't count on this room in the future, but you really need to rest right now." My mother slept out in the Critical Care waiting room on a couch.

As I drifted off to sleep, I remembered an experience a member of our church had had back in Provo. Greg Beckstrom came down with a bad cold that quickly turned into pneumonia. Within a few days he was on the edge between this life and the next. He then had a visionlike experience: he was basically given the choice to live or to die. He realized that the choice to die was not a terrible one because he would eventually be reunited with his family, and time goes slowly in this life but not in the next. But if he chose to live, he and his wife could raise their family together. He chose life and recovered quickly. I wondered if David would have this same experience, and I hoped he would choose life, so I whispered "choose life" occasionally to him so he would know my vote.

I also know several people who, while sleeping, have had a visit or encounter with someone who has just died. David himself has had such an experience. I was afraid as I let myself fall into unconsciousness. I didn't want David to come to me in a dream to say good-bye because I didn't want him to die. I slept fitfully. At 6:00 A.M. I woke up to check on David. He was still alive, so I went back to sleep.

The second day, Wednesday, was grim. While I was napping again in the staff sleeping room, Dr. Shin, the surgeon, and my mother awoke me. He sat on the chair, my mother sat on the end of the bed. I left the room dark. They had operated on David Tuesday evening, and now Wednesday morning, they operated again. Dr. Shin gave me his latest postsurgery prognosis. He said he did not have a good feeling about David's chances. David's neck was so swollen that Dr. Shin worried the bacteria had spread there. Much of the skin on his arm was gone, and the bacteria seemed to have spread down his side. The surgeons were trying to anticipate where it would go next. They cut away anything that looked infected. They would probably have to amputate his arm and any other limb that became infected. Worse yet, his heart was acting strangely, and Dr. Shin feared that the bacteria might be there already. If so, David would certainly die.

Hope diminished. Although we celebrated when we reached the twenty-four-hour mark, now I felt I should really face the idea of David dying. It was at this point that, in my own mind, I began referring to Dr. Shin as Dr. Grim, since he always seemed to be bringing me bad news, always preparing me for the worst.

David's parents, Leon and Beth Cowles, arrived from Portland, and the hospital volunteers helped them find a hotel for the night. My neighbor Craig came to the hospital to represent my brothers and sister who were hundreds of miles away. At my request, my parents again brought the children to say hello to David, but I hesitated taking them into his room because their father looked too swollen and sick—not a great sight to linger in your mind forever. I decided Steven (8) and Marissa (3) should stay in the waiting room. I didn't know whether twelve-year-old Robby could handle it. He had been quite distressed the night before when he saw David on the verge of his first operation. I gave Robby the choice, and he decided to remain in the waiting room. Kathryn (15) and Cristie (17) came with me to talk to their father. All David could do was blink his eyes in partial recognition. It was very hard for us all.

That night we all went home to sleep. David had now been in the hospital thirty-six hours, and I had yet to sleep anywhere but the hospital. I slept on a hide-a-bed in the family room. No one would sleep in the bed David had gotten sick in. We were afraid even to go in to change the sheets. We prayed again as a family, and we all tried to sleep. As I lay down after my own long, heartfelt prayer, I used all my concentration to clear a spirit of heavy darkness that seemed determined to overcome me. Demons floated in my mind, and I had no peace. I heard Cristie locked in the bathroom, crying. But I couldn't move to go and comfort her. It took all my energy to keep from sinking into the darkness assailing me. "Heavenly Father, please help me," I whispered over and over.

The next morning, I looked in my closet and noticed David's Christmas presents—new shoes, shirts, expensive Dockers, some books. I thought, I wonder if I can take these back. My father and I sat down on the edge of his bed and talked. It sounded as if the doctors were going to amputate limbs wherever the bacteria spread. Even then, David would probably not live. Dad and I discussed life insurance, our finances, and how I would support the family. In my mind I was already thinking of ways we could slash our expenses so we could live on just my salary: quit piano lessons, have the children live at home during college years, pay off the mortgage and other loans with the life insurance money, sew our own clothes, live off our stored food, cancel cable TV. I even admitted I might consider getting married again. "But only to someone rich," I facetiously said.

But the timing seemed all wrong. David was only forty. In his teaching I have seen him influence many people to be more righteous and spiritual, more tolerant of others, more responsive to God's will. I've read students' notes to him, and I see the guidance he gives many who face intellectual-spiritual crises, as he did earlier in his life. I know the strong influence he has on his own sons and daughters. And on me, for heaven's sake. I remember bargaining with God: "If you need him, take him. But there are very few people here on earth who can do what David does. I know he can do much more to serve you."

I finally decided that if the Lord chose to let David die, I would let him go. But if God chose to spare him, I would do everything I could do to help David live.

How Do You Spell
Necrotizing Fasciitis?

After only a few days of being around the hospital, I had developed a new medical vocabulary. Morphine, dopamine, hematology, nephrology, subcutaneous fascia, systemic shock, necrosis, debridement, pseudomonas, etc. I was learning to talk in medicalese—I could even understand the doctors and ask intelligent questions.

I could now look at a monitor and see David's heart rate, his blood pressure, and his oxygen-in-blood reading. I could see whether his kidneys were working by glancing at the urine flow. I watched a waste vessel fill up with yellow and reddish liquid as a vacuum tube down his nose cleaned out his stomach.

His blood pressure readings interested me most. The machine constantly read David's blood pressure by a catheter in his chest. He was still relying on dopamine to pull the blood from the outer reaches of his body to concentrate most of the blood in his heart area. This made his toes start to turn purple on the tips as they were deprived of enough blood to keep the tissue strong.

David's toes may have looked terrible, but these were the least of my worries. I had called my insurance company, and they gave approval for fourteen days in the hospital to begin with. I knew David's stay would be much, much longer. They also told me we would be responsible for 10 percent of the cost up to $1,500 per calendar year (of course with our bad timing, he entered the hospital the last week of December), and then we would have to pay 2 percent of the total cost. The insurance people also told me that our insurance cap was $1,000,000, which sounded far away at the time, but deep inside I worried. I even found myself wondering that if David was going to die, maybe he could get on with it and not linger on into a whole new calendar year of deductions. But I repented of that thinking.

By now I was discovering more about this flesh-destroying disease, and I always carried around a piece of paper with the correct spelling— NECROTIZING FASCIITIS—since I was asked a lot. The doctors and I tried to figure out how David contracted the disease. The only explanation we could come up with was that it entered his body through the small cut on his finger from the suitcase zipper. There were no other breaks in his body, and the finger had become infected the day after David had nicked it.

The bacteria strain attacking David is actually a rather common variety found all around us, but our bodies usually fight it off. This time the streptococcus A bacteria turned aggressive and spread at enormously fast rates—in David's case it spread an inch an hour. Streptoccocus A bacteria cause well-known diseases such as scarlet fever, but a more virulent strain causes streptococcal toxic shock syndrome, and sometimes this leads to necrotizing fasciitis.

The tabloid name "flesh-eating bacteria" scares a lot of people. It is purposefully shocking. But then, the disease itself is shockingly devastating. The bacteria destroys the fascia, which is the membrane around the muscles. One nurse explained fascia to me this way: "You know when you take the skin off chicken, there is a thin membrane attaching the skin to the meat. That is the fascia." Necrotizing means dead. Dead membrane. It is a rather ugly picture.

I wondered, how do people get flesh-eating bacteria? How does it spread? What are the possibilities of me getting it? How do you know you have it? What can we do to prevent this disease? Are we going to have an epidemic?

Case histories show that people have contracted necrotizing fasciitis in many different ways. Some through a small cut, some through surgical wounds, some after dental surgery, some through chicken pox lesions, some from deep bruises, and some have no specific point of entry. It usually spreads through an opening in the skin. Yet invasive strep infections are uncommon because our bodies usually fight off these bacteria.

We worried that the rest of us at home were at risk of contracting this disease too. If anyone would have "caught" this from David, it would have been me, since I slept next to him and took care of him when he first became ill. But then I found out that the bacteria is everywhere around all of us anyway, and that we as family members were no more at risk than anyone else. Necrotizing fasciitis is an infectious disease, but only very rarely will someone become infected. And these people usually have a low general immunity.

Some of the hospital workers were apprehensive about working with David because they didn't know how contagious he was. One physical therapist expressed her apprehensions at working on someone with this scary and rare disease:

> Over the previous several months, more and more people had been victims of the "flesh-eating bacteria," and now there was one here at Presbyterian Hospital. Word was that our physical therapy department would play a big part in the care of the man in room 380 CCU. There was discussion about what the dangers were in "getting" the much dreaded bacteria—so little was known. Several staff spoke of their families' fear for their safety.

> At dinner one night at my parents' house, we spoke of the man in CCU. Although compassionate for this man's situation, they expressed their fears when I told them that I would be trained to work with this man. If everyone decided not to get involved, then who would be left? I would want to know that someone would be there for one of my family members, and I felt that God's hand would keep those of us who would work with this man safe in his hands.

There are some common symptoms of this uncommon disease. Most people who contract necrotizing fasciitis feel intense pain described as muscle aches. David's pains were so intense that he could hardly endure them. Many have flulike symptoms such as diarrhea, vomiting, and the chills. Sometimes the person registers a fever, but David never did. In more advanced cases, the infected area becomes swollen and red, then later blue, then purple, then black when the tissue is dead. Almost everyone goes into shock with low blood pressure, and the shock and toxins from the bacteria cause some organs to shut down, such as the kidneys or the liver or the lungs. If they are not treated promptly, most people die immediately, and you can see why.

Some people have a milder case of necrotizing fasciitis, one that can be carefully monitored in the doctor's office over time. David's was nothing like this. By the time a spot showed on his skin and the doctors could finally diagnose the disease, the bacteria had spread far, his whole body was shutting down, and he was close to death. His was a very advanced case.

Who gets this disease? The bacteria are not very picky. People of any age group, any gender, and any race. People who are chronically ill, and people who seem otherwise healthy. Some researchers wonder if people who contract necrotizing fasciitis have a suppressed immune system. Some suggest the use of medicines such as ibuprofen might make someone susceptible to these infections. Ibuprofen suppresses the immune system to help prevent swelling, but it might also suppress the immune system enough that the body doesn't fight off this kind of streptococcus. And yes, David was taking ibuprofen and another anti-inflammatory medicine the month before he got sick. Yet our daughter who has juvenile rheumatoid arthritis has been taking anti-inflammatories for years, and she did not contract this disease. Could we have prevented this disease? If we had it to do over again, we would have washed his cut with soap and water and put an antibacterial salve and a bandage on his finger.

Lucien Bouchard, a political leader in Canada, came down with necrotizing fasciitis in 1994 and lost his leg to it. In 1990, Jim Henson, who created the Muppets, died of a group A streptococcal toxic shock syndrome that began as strep pneumonia. Necrotizing fasciitis has been documented since around 1900, and it is not a new strain of bacteria. But some wonder if the strain has become more virulent and if it attacks more often than in past years. It certainly has received more publicity lately. A year after we returned from London in 1994, the British tabloids began to report several new cases of this strange disease they dubbed "flesh-eating bacteria." You can't fault them for not being vivid. The name has stuck, and by now many people have heard of the popular name of the disease, and it scares us all.

Is there an epidemic of necrotizing fasciitis? Well, the number of people who have contracted this disease has probably increased, but the disease is still not widespread. Other diseases caused by group A streptococcus such as scarlet fever have had large epidemics, but the necrotizing fasciitis bacteria is not spreading wildly. Some would say only the reporting has increased. The chances of catching this disease are very, very small. You have a better chance of getting struck by lightning.

As we all learned more about the disease, we realized that now David had a much greater chance of catching something from us than we had of catching something from him.

Support from Home

Although these first two days were very dark, we were not alone in praying for David. Word spread quickly. The members of my parents' congregation knew David was sick because it all began during my grandmother's funeral at their chapel. My Waite relatives all knew because they were at the funeral too. David's parents had spread the word to their friends in Portland, Oregon, and family throughout Utah. We seemed to have one representative from each group that we could call and pass on news to. Mickey Bladh, a high school friend who was a nurse at Presbyterian Intercommunity, became our local informer; people called her for updates. My Uncle Richard passed on the news to my Waite relatives.

Back in Utah, Bruce Bryan, the head of our local church congregation, spread the news. I originally caught him at his office in the middle of end-of-the-year business, and I asked him to ask the other church members to pray for David. It took less than an hour for all eighty families to receive the news, and so within minutes our entire congregation was praying for our family. In several cases young children made sure their families never prayed without mentioning David.

Then on Wednesday night something quite magical happened. The fax machine at the nurses' station rolled off page after page of notes from members of our congregation.

All in all our friends sent thirty pages of fax messages that night.

"Is this guy some kind of a celebrity or something?" The puzzled nurses asked.

"No, we're just normal people. We just have a lot of people who love us," I said, with pride in my congregation.

As I carried the faxes around with me Wednesday night, I felt that my church friends were with me. The next morning, a Federal Express messenger brought a large envelope full of letters for our children. Evidently, my daughters' friends went all over Provo collecting letters from Cristie's and Kathryn's close friends. It was holiday time, and almost everyone was in town and at home. Wow, it was comforting to have so many written messages of support from a lot of our friends.

. . .

By this time, our neighbor and colleague, Beth Hedengren, had called people who had called people who had called people until the whole English Department at Brigham Young University knew about my condition. The news shocked everyone, and the entire department began to pray for my recovery. On Wednesday morning, Doug Thayer, a colleague, gathered about fifteen people together in the department office for a prayer. This was in the middle of the semester break, but some people were still around in their offices.

On Thursday, grades were due, so a lot of professors showed up. By now the department office had become the central gathering point for sharing information and concern. Usually at this time of year, people drop off grades and leave quickly to enjoy more holiday time away from work. This time people just hung around the halls to find out how I was doing. That morning about thirty-five members of the English faculty and several colleagues from other departments gathered in the word processing center to pray together. Colleagues who disagreed deeply about professional issues felt unaccustomed unity at this time.

Though the BYU English Department faculty tends to be somewhat less contentious than English departments at other large universities, we have our professional disagreements, too. At present the theoretical underpinnings of our entire discipline is undergoing radical revision. Invigorated by many new perspectives and critical approaches to the study of language and literature, English departments everywhere are engaged in deeply emotional rethinking regarding the nature of the profession and the future directions of the discipline.

As in other places, BYU's English faculty divides into groups who espouse very different philosophies regarding these issues. We fit into a lot of different categories: formalists, rhetoricians, linguists, new historicists, deconstructionists, Marxists, multiculturalists, moralists, feminists, Americanists, British specialists, and about any other kind of -ists you can think of. I myself have edited and cowritten a successful textbook that tries to help beginning literature students

47

make sense of this bewildering array of critical perspectives. Our faculty, typical of English departments everywhere, seems to divide into many overlapping and often competing groups. Older versus younger, American literature specialists versus British literature enthusiasts, language faculty versus literature experts, traditionalists versus revisionists.

At times even faculty members at religious institutions such as ours seem to forget the beliefs that bind them, and engage in rancorous disagreements. I believe this happens more easily in English departments than in some others because of the personal and moral implications of everything we teach. In English departments, how one approaches his or her discipline has everything to do with who one is and what he or she believes at the most personal levels. Sometimes we lose track of deeper, more important values in arguing for positions that seem morally self-evident to us but which may seem wrong-headed to someone else with equally cherished and morally based ideas.

However, on this bleak December day, professors from every philosophical bent knelt together in the word processing center. Jay Fox, the department chair, asked my longtime friend and colleague Phil Snyder to offer a prayer for everyone. The word processing center is usually a busy place full of computers and printers, photocopy machines and telephones, secretaries, faculty mailboxes, and paper supplies. A lot of people greet each other and have short conversations at the mailboxes every day. This day, though, the room became a holy place, and thirty-five people with deep religious beliefs and strong personal emotions reverently and unitedly prayed for a close colleague. After a long and moving prayer and many tears, the members of this group quietly dispersed to private places to pray individually.

Many of my friends continued to make spiritual connections during this time. For example, Peter Sorensen, another colleague and close friend, wrote about his experiences later that day:

I had prayed on-and-off for a whole day, and it was during the second night that I had the dream-vision. I was standing in the doorway of the word processing center down the hall from my office in the humanities building, and I saw Dave standing there, without his glasses but with his silly Russian cap on. I said, "It's nice to have you back!" and he responded, "It's good to be back!" It was such a vivid dream that when I awoke, waking seemed a dream by comparison. I knew I had seen Dave alive and recovered from his illness. That day, after the dream, I met colleagues in the halls who had somber looks and dark tones in their voices. They discussed how slim Dave's chances were. I told everyone not to doubt but to have faith, because Dave wasn't going to die. I don't know why such a thing happened to me, but I had never been more convinced of anything in my life.

Other department members had moving and spiritual experiences of their own. For a time, at least, it seemed that the issues that had divided our department completely disappeared. Several letters (of many) I received from department members—some of which I was in no condition to read until weeks later—give a sense of what was happening back home.

One male colleague, a longtime friend, wrote: "I've shed more tears these last few days than I have in a year—not bitter or even sorrowful ones so much as tears of faith, pleading, anxiety, and (occasionally) gratitude."

One of our more senior faculty members described some of the positive effects my illness had on the department as a whole:

We have all had you on our minds, in our conversations, and in our prayers more than you might dare to believe. And, yes, all that has had a good effect on the department. It feels to me that we are less grim and antagonistic toward one another than we have been. So consider your suffering, though terrible, at least beneficial. Certainly, all our problems are not solved, and the distance between older and younger faculty is still considerable, but, at least temporarily, worrying about you has restored some sense of perspective. . . . You have helped us as a department. I hope we have helped, and can yet help, you.

Another colleague wrote:

Singlehandedly (and in absentia, I might add), you've done an incredible amount of bridge-building within the department, bringing us closer together and helping us understand what really matters. As Phil observed, however, we must have been truly accursed to have warranted such a wake-up message. And it is a tragedy, on some levels at least, that you must suffer for us. I'm sure, however, that in the economy of the Lord, you and your family will reap immediate, more enduring, more sacred blessings—blessings that will somehow justify your experience.

In retrospect, he was right.

Perhaps Jay Fox, our department chair, summed it all up best: "There has been an outpouring of love and concern from everyone here. I think you could have come up with something a little less dramatic to pull us all together."

Life or Death?

Thursday morning I went to the hospital knowing I might have to let David go. I decided that if he was obviously not going to make it, I wouldn't hang on to him selfishly (not that I had much choice). After my first night's sleep in a few days, I was more willing to say "Thy will be done" in my prayers.

When I arrived at the hospital, the Critical Care waiting room was filled with people who were there for David: my parents-in-law, their friends, and Eva and Danny Thron. My mother and father traded being at the hospital and being at home with the children. This morning my father brought me to the hospital because my mother took the children to get tested for strep, just to make sure no one else had David's disease. At the hospital I didn't want to talk to anyone. I just wanted to be with David and see if he had the will to live, but he was in the hyperbaric chamber and I couldn't see him for a little while. I passed the time by wandering some halls alone.

After a bit, Dr. Saketkhoo, David's Critical Care doctor, came in to give us an update. Much to my surprise, his news was good. David was doing much better. He said David's body was stabilizing and that they had lowered his dosage of dopamine, so he was producing more blood pressure on his own. His kidneys were beginning to work better. His blood looked good, and best of all, the bacteria did not seem to be in his heart or any other organ—only in the soft tissue under his skin. They had lanced and drained his badly swollen neck, and there was no sign of the bacteria there, either.

I was prepared for bad news but not for this good news. Hope flowed again, and I looked forward to celebrating the forty-eight-hour mark. I walked back to the hyperbaric chamber to see how the session was going.

David was doing well, said one of the respiratory therapists. He told me David had reacted favorably to some music on the radio, and that somehow he had communicated to them that he liked jazz best. Music. Of course. David loved music. He had begun college as a piano major. He still played every day, wrote songs to express his emotions, and listened to many kinds of music constantly. He was apparently conscious enough to be moved by music. I asked the therapists if they could play tapes in the chamber, and they said yes.

Then I got a great idea. I drove home and grabbed David's headphones, his portable tape player, and the twenty or so tapes he had brought to listen to on our vacation. If anything could help heal him, music could. I left a quick note for my mother (who was still at the doctor's office with the children) that said, "David is a little better today. I came home to get his tapes. See you."

Back at the hospital I didn't stop to talk to anyone. I wanted to see David. I had a feeling I wouldn't have to let him go after all, but I wanted to see for myself. I walked back to David's room, and when I got close, I could feel the full presence of his personality. He still had tubes everywhere, including down his throat to help him breathe, so he couldn't talk to me, but his eyes and hand-squeezes expressed much.

I asked David the question I had been mulling over for a day, even though I already knew the answer: "David, do you want to live?"

"Are you crazy? Of course I do," his eyes told me. I could tell he had not considered death this whole time.

"Well, that's good, because you are going to live. I am proud of you for fighting off this infection so well."

David tried to move his right hand, but could not because it was wrapped up and strapped down. He motioned with his left hand for a pen.

"I love you," he scrawled with the wrong writing hand. I have a good husband.

"I love you," I responded.

Next he scrawled, "Time?" He obviously had no idea how long he had been out.

Finally he wrote "pillow," meaning, as he explained later, "Please find me a comfortable pillow like the one I have at home. This lousy hospital thing is driving me crazy."

As David drifted off in sleep, I slipped his headphones over his head and turned on the Beatles.

. . .

I had mixed feelings about dying, though the idea that I might die never occurred to me until my survival was fairly certain. But I am not afraid to die. In fact, I am eager to see what the next life is like.

A few years ago I was assigned by my church to visit the Beckstrom family each month. In our church every family is assigned someone to look after them. During the time I visited the Beckstrom family, the father, Greg, became very ill. While he was lying unconscious in the hospital, he and his wife, Brenda, together had a vividly remembered near-death experience. Greg had gone to the hospital with a mysterious disease his doctors could only describe as "atypical pneumonia." Eventually his condition became so serious that Greg lost consciousness for several days. Brenda, a registered nurse who worked at the hospital, spent many hours sitting with her husband and helping monitor the many machines hooked up to him.

One day the Critical Care nurse asked Brenda if she could keep an eye on Greg for a few minutes. The nurse had to go to another section of the hospital to help bring a new patient to Critical Care. Brenda readily agreed, and the other nurse left. Suddenly Brenda felt an overpowering sense that Greg was about to crash. A few seconds later the monitors registering his respiration rate, heart rate, and oxygenation dropped rapidly and dangerously. Alarms began sounding. Greg's breathing suddenly stopped altogether. He was clearly dying.

Brenda had helped resuscitate many patients in her duties as a nurse. Jumping up to begin those procedures on her husband was second nature to her—like reaching out to steady a child who was falling.

But as she rose from her chair, Brenda felt a physical force that literally pushed her back into the chair, as if a pair of irresistibly strong hands held her down. She felt an overpowering sense of calm and an assurance that everything would be all right. She felt the presence of her husband completely engulf her, as if he were holding every part of her, physically and spiritually. She felt completely safe and confident.

Then Brenda heard Greg's voice in her mind, as clearly as if he had spoken aloud, though his lips never moved. "I think it's time to go now," he said. Brenda could feel his spirit moving on. Greg said later that he felt if anyone had asked him to do even the slightest thing at that time, he could not have done it. His

53

mortal strength was completely gone, and he felt empty of energy or will. He knew his life was ending.

"The kids and I will miss you," Brenda heard herself say in her mind, "but whatever you decide will be okay."

Then they both heard a third voice, kind and calming. "It won't be for long, anyway," it said. They both felt the voice's assurance that whatever happened would be right and good.

Suddenly Brenda heard Greg gulp a huge breath of air—his first for some time. Though he remained unconscious, Greg's vital signs all quickly rose to their previous levels.

At that moment the door opened and two leaders of our congregation entered quickly. "What's wrong?" One man said, "We both just knew suddenly that Greg was in crisis, and we rushed over here as fast as we could."

"Don't worry," said Brenda, still glowing inside from her experience. "Everything's fine now."

Later, when Greg recovered consciousness, Brenda found him crying. "What's wrong?" she asked.

"All my life," he said, "I've wanted to have a great spiritual experience—one that would assure me that God is there and that I'm doing the right things. I feel as if I'd had such an experience, but I'm afraid I missed it."

Brenda smiled. "What do you remember?" she asked.

Greg's memory, hazier now, knew that he had felt his spirit leaving. He distinctly recalled hearing voices, and he remembered the words exactly as Brenda did.

"But who was the other person in the room?" he asked. "The one who said, 'It won't be for long, anyway?' And what did he mean by that?"

Brenda explained what had happened.

"You were obviously given a choice," Brenda said. "You could move on to the next life, or you could remain here with us. You chose to come back and raise your family, at least for a while. And I'll be eternally grateful that you did."

Once Greg had made that decision, his recovery was rapid and complete, to the profound joy of his family and friends.

I remembered Greg's story in the early days of my recovery. Had I been offered the same choice, I'm not sure what I would have done. I love my life here, but the next one entices me with the promise of new knowledge and understanding, expanded abilities, reunion with loved ones who have died, and God's presence *and love. However, I also know the grief and hardships that my death would cause my family and others. I felt in many ways as the apostle Paul did: "For to me to live is Christ, and to die is gain. . . . For I am in a strait betwixt the two, having a desire to depart, and to be with Christ; which is far better: Nevertheless to abide in the flesh is more needful for you" (Philippians 1:21, 23–24).*

As it turned out, however, I was never offered that choice. It seems to have been made instead by those who prayed for my recovery.

. . .

Later, a member of a book group I belong to told me that as she prayed for David, she received an overpowering spiritual assurance that his life would be spared because of all the prayers offered on his behalf by righteous people. My sister, Wendy, now back in Arizona with her family, told me she could hardly do anything for a week except pray for our family. It occupied all of her time and thoughts. Children from our church added "bless Brother Cowles" to every one of their prayers. Beth Hedengren told me she had a constant litany for many days: "Bless David, bless Delys, bless their family." Beth also told me her thirteen-year-old son felt very calm during his prayers. "I feel that Brother Cowles is going to be okay," he said. David's father, while giving him a healing blessing in the hospital, felt a calm and absolute assurance that David would be all right.

It seems that God knew exactly what he was doing.

Praying for the Right Arm

Thursday afternoon Dr. Shin, ready for the day's surgery, introduced me to Dr. Britto, a brilliant plastic surgeon. Dr. Shin told me he had asked Dr. Britto to join him because they would probably have to amputate David's right arm. This took me by surprise.

"But he is a pianist. Remember in your operation that he is a pianist."

"I thought he was an English professor."

"Well, playing the piano isn't his profession. It's his great love, though. He has composed many pieces. He expresses his deepest emotions through his music. It's how he keeps his sanity, he often says. Remember he is a pianist."

I prayed hard during the operation that David would recover fully and that he would be able to keep his arm. After the operation the surgeons told us that after some disagreement they had decided to leave his arm for today, but that they would reevaluate again tomorrow. The normal way to treat necrotizing fasciitis is to amputate whatever body part is infected so the bacteria can't spread. It's generally the only way to save the life of the patient. What is the use of saving the arm just to have the patient die? But on the other hand, if the patient lives, wouldn't the use of his arm enhance his life? The surgeons were walking a thin line.

Even more frightening, though, the bacteria was still spreading. Dr. Shin had expected it to go down David's legs or to his back, but he saw a red streak across David's abdomen and traced the infection to his left side now. Dr. Britto said he had performed many operations, but the large amounts of dead jellylike tissue they removed from David's abdomen had made him feel sick. Dr. Shin still only gave David a 10-percent chance of living, but I could tell David was going to survive.

At home I discussed David's arm with the family. I felt funny praying for his arm at first. I felt as if I had already been offered a banquet with David staying alive, and now I was ungratefully demanding dessert. But my father reminded us that we should pray for the things we need. "For heaven's sakes, Delys, David needs his arm." So we prayed for it. I had never prayed for a specific body part before, but I spent the night half sleeping and half pleading for David's arm. Around midnight I called Eva Thron and told her about David's arm. She turned on a tape of David's compositions and had a frank and deeply emotional talk with God about the need for his arm.

Three times the surgeons went in to amputate David's arm, and every time they decided it had enough healthy tissue to leave it. Even so, his arm had lost most of the skin and much of the underlying tissue. He was missing great clumps of skin and tissue and muscle over his entire torso; only about half the skin on his upper body remained. But his body was getting stronger and fighting the disease.

By now, David was so doped up with morphine that he was almost always unconscious. I continued to put on his headphones and played REM, U2, Nanci Griffith, and the Indigo Girls. He rarely opened his eyes now. In the hyperbaric chamber I had the hospital staff play David's tapes over the system to relax him. One respiratory therapist says he named a U2 song "David's Song" because he first heard it in the hyperbaric chamber with David.

After several days of David's deep unconsciousness, the doctors decided to try to bring him back. They lowered the morphine dose and waited. He didn't regain consciousness. We waited another day. Still no consciousness. The nurses guessed that David's mind was just trying to protect itself from the trauma of the situation by turning off. "I'd do the same in his position," I added.

So the nurse told me to talk to him and try to bring him out of his unconsciousness. I started out by talking about literary theory, his favorite topic at the university. Wrong choice. Too intense intellectually. I then started talking about the room and the trees outside. "That will do for now," the nurse said as she ushered me out.

· · ·

My first experience with complete consciousness took the medical staff by surprise. I suddenly awoke to find myself in a bed. A nurse was holding my right arm up in the air to change the dressing. I looked over at it and was horrified to see not my arm, but a shocking mess of blood, muscle, tissue—indeed everything but skin.

I remember formulating my first question calmly and carefully: "What in the world happened to my arm?" I asked the nurse. She seemed shocked that I was alert enough to ask such a question. I wasn't supposed to see what had happened to me until I had been properly prepared. I didn't understand until later the panic my sudden awakening caused.

Nurses hurried off to fetch the doctor. The nurse holding my arm brought it down where I could not see it. "You've been very ill," she said. "Don't worry about anything. You're going to be all right."

"Oh," I said with relief. I thought, I'm going to be all right. I guess I can go back to sleep. But before I could, one of the nurses who had left returned to tell me about the hospital's counseling services. Did I want to see a psychiatrist? she asked frantically. Would I like a visit from the chaplain? The questions seemed unnecessary; I had already forgotten my arm as I slipped back into unconsciousness. "No," I mumbled as everything around me blurred. "Why should I want to see any of them?"

Meet the Press

By Thursday afternoon David had beat the odds and lived forty-eight hours. I was ready to celebrate because I felt he had turned the corner, but the doctors cautioned us that his chances of survival were still very slim. Still only 10 percent. But to me this was a 10-percent chance with some major hope behind it.

Late that afternoon on Thursday, December 29, Dr. Tuddenham, David's infectious-disease doctor, told us that the story had hit the press. Dr. Tuddenham had just held a news conference in the hospital about our situation. The public relations representative for the hospital asked me if I would like to talk to members of the press. I said no. I knew people were interested in the disease, not in us, and I refused to become part of a possible circus. Besides, it would be very hard talking to people about my husband, who was still close to death. On top of that, I cried a lot in the hospital, usually when nobody could see. My eyes were puffy, and I looked like a person who hadn't slept for a while. Maybe because I hadn't.

Now, every time I left the hospital, there was a news reporter and a TV camera giving the latest update outside the hospital. I walked by smiling to myself, keeping my anonymity, knowing they had no idea I was THE WIFE.

Thursday night, though, I lost it.

I was sitting in the Critical Care waiting room away from David so he could rest. I was talking with my in-laws when my father-in-law said, "There is a TV camera outside the door." I looked through the waiting room windows and saw nothing, so I walked out the door into the hall. Indeed, there was a TV camera with its lens up against the window of the door leading to my husband's Critical Care Unit. I was enraged. How could a cameraman be so snoopy and rude as to come right up to David's room and stick his lens in the window? I figured he would walk twenty feet and start filming my husband in his bed next. I was furious. And when I get furious, I get bold.

"Excuse me, what are you doing sticking your lens in that window? How dare you invade our family's privacy this way. How dare you come with a camera right outside the Critical Care waiting area where all the family is. Get out. You cannot do this to people."

Then I noticed he was actually being led around by a hospital administrator. This really upset me as I thought about it later. When the cameraman left and went to the locked back entrance of the Critical Care Unit, I was worried the administrator was going to let him into my husband's room. I ran in the front doors and found several of David's doctors there.

"Do you know there is a television news camera right outside that door this very minute?" I said almost hysterically. "Can you believe they would walk right up to someone's room in the hospital and poke their camera in the window? Can you believe a TV cameraman would be taking pictures right outside the waiting room where all the families are? This is the rudest thing I have ever seen."

"Don't worry, we had the curtain pulled on your husband's room," one doctor consoled.

I could tell they were in on it. This infuriated me, and my father-in-law joined in the heated complaint. Then they told me that they had held a press conference earlier because "people have the right to know about this," as one doctor explained.

"But I don't want my children to be watching television only to hear that their father is near death, with pictures to prove it."

Now, as I think back on it, I realize that I objected to the lack of personal dignity afforded this situation. To the media, this was just a monster bacteria attacking its next victim, and I refused to fuel the supermarket-tabloid mentality. There was much more dignity in this situation, but I could tell this was not the story the press was after.

Later that night I watched the news programs to see what they would say. Much to my surprise, one doctor said on camera the patient's name was "David Cowles, a professor at Brigham Young University." So much for anonymity. Because they didn't have any pictures of David, they showed a lot of pictures of other victims of necrotizing fasciitis, and they were scary.

Since the pictures they showed didn't include the victims' faces, they appeared to be of David, though none were.

My children watched some of the broadcasts and moaned loudly every time someone mispronounced our name (which was every time). Our last name, Cowles, looks like it begins with the sound of "cow," but really you pronounce it as if it didn't have a "w," rhyming with "souls." Actually this is rather useful because at home, I can always tell when a telephone call is from someone selling something—the person always mispronounces our name!

That night I rethought the media problem. I remember when the Watkins family in our church congregation lost their son, Brian. The family was in New York City for the U.S. Open tennis tournament, and they decided to go to a restaurant. As they stood on the subway platform, a group of young men robbed them at knifepoint. Then a tussle began, and one of the young men fatally stabbed Brian, who was trying to protect his mother. There they were, in a strange city, having to face this great tragedy with no friends around, and also having to deal with a curious press. I remember that when they came home, reporters were always hanging around on their street. The Watkinses handled the situation by holding press conferences so they could talk to everyone at once. I remember how uncomfortable it was for them and for us as their friends to grieve at the funeral with so many cameras around. But they handled everything with dignity and grace. I used them as my model.

.   .   .

Had I been in any condition to recognize what was happening, all the public attention my disease and I were getting would have surprised me (and perhaps annoyed me) greatly. I have always marveled at the way members of the press sometimes pester victims and their families, hovering like vultures around a not-quite-dead body, reaching in when they think they can get away with it to tear off a bit of flesh. While I recognize the vital importance of a robust and uncensored press in a free society, I also often regret the lack of dignity American reporters too often give those they so insistently cover.

My family and I have felt a certain responsibility to talk to the press about our experiences—from basically the same motives that have resulted in this book. We feel this story is not ours alone. We know thousands of people were involved, directly and indirectly. If they helped make a miracle, we owe it to them to tell the story. They deserve to hear it all, and they deserve to be honored for their contributions. So we have always tried to respond with good grace whenever news people have asked us about our experience.

But we have always wanted to tell what we consider to be the real story: how many people from many different religions and backgrounds came together to help create a miracle. The human story, the story of faith and good will, is the story that matters. In later weeks, when we were able to be selective about which reporters we invited to talk with us and cover my progress, we met many humane, sensitive reporters who allowed us to tell this story of faith and joy.

But during those first days the reporters seemed interested only in stories saying: Look! Here's another horrible, frightening disease! A bacteria that is actually eating away some poor person's skin! Yes, this horrifying disease really exists, and it might get you next!

So when the press hounded my family and treated our suffering as an excuse for frightening people with tabloid-style terrors, we naturally felt some resentment. Had I been able, I would have been leading the charge to banish the vultures trying to turn us into an undignified and freakish media meal.

. . .

David and I were not strangers to the media. We had both had experiences with television interviews in Chicago when we were graduate students. We had just bought a townhouse in a new cooperative housing development on the south side of Chicago. Since David was studying at the University of Chicago for his Ph.D., we decided to live close to the university. After a year in married-student housing, we moved to Woodlawn, just south of Hyde Park and the university. Almost all the residents of Woodlawn were African American, and when this housing development opened up, the government agencies involved with financing it wanted more of an ethnic mix. Several families of other races bought into the cooperative, and it happened that we were the first to move in.

The opening of the housing development became a media event, and we were picked to talk to reporters, along with an African American family. Both wives were eight months pregnant, so we made quite a sight. We spent an entire day posing for pictures and talking to news reporters. That night I watched some of the news broadcasts to see what they did with the interviews. From half-hour interviews, editors choose 10- to 20-second bytes to show on the news. Unfortunately, out of context, my 10 seconds on one station made no sense, and I looked like a fool. The next day at work, my boss said, "I saw you on the news last night. Nice interview, but just what were you trying to say?"

So I was skeptical of news reporters and the power of editors. I didn't want to appear foolish again.

But then I thought about something else. There is a lot of goodness in the world that rarely gets reported. Stories about people acting out of kindness and love usually don't sell many papers or bring in high ratings. Also, religious people are often portrayed in the American media as close-minded and brainless. I began to feel an obligation to speak publicly about the good things that were happening to us: the wonderful care in the hospital, the kindness of the hospital volunteers, the support of our church, and the religious healing energy of many people from many religions praying for us. I discussed with my father the pros and cons of talking to the press. I decided late Thursday night that I would talk to people, but only if I could focus on the good, not the bizarre.

The next day, I checked in on David and went to the waiting room to talk to my parents-in-law. Much to my surprise, a social worker from the hospital came into the waiting room and asked for me. She wanted to talk to me about our situation and how our family was handling the stress of my husband's illness. Then the hospital chaplain came to comfort me and to see if she could help in any way. I appreciated their concern, but I realized that the doctors probably set these interviews up because of my outburst the day before. I chuckled inside.

One of the hospital volunteers handed me a note that said Denise from the hospital's public relations office wanted me to call her.

"I've had a lot of newspeople calling me today. I am getting lots of calls from Utah, especially," she informed me. "In the last few minutes I have heard from two radio stations in Salt Lake City. I assume you don't want to talk to them."

"Actually I think I am willing to talk to them, if it is just on the phone."

So, I took the elevator down to her office, thinking the whole time that my life as an anonymous person was about to end. I called both radio stations from Denise's office, which was nice since most of my phone conversations the last few days had been on a busy pay phone next to the noisy waiting room.

The first reporter asked if he could record the interview, and I said yes.

Then he asked if I would grant an interview to their Los Angeles television affiliate so they could beam it to the Utah station. I still had visions of the TV camera rudely poking around the hospital the night before. I said, "No, they wouldn't ask me the questions I want to answer."

After giving them an update about David, and after thanking people in Utah for their prayers and letters, I called the next station. They asked the same questions, but then they said, "Would you grant an interview to one of our television news reporters if we flew one down."

I said, "Well, I look terrible. I've been sitting in a hospital for four days with hardly any sleep, and I don't even have any makeup or a brush with me. I'd rather just talk over the phone."

"We would really like to send someone right now."

"Are you sure people are actually interested in this? I hate to break it to you, but we are just normal people."

"A lot of people love you here, and everyone is interested."

"Okay, I'll do it."

This would be a great chance to say thank you to everyone praying for us back home. I went back to the waiting room and found our friend Eva. "Help, I'm going to do a television interview. Do you have any makeup I can borrow? Do you have a brush?" I thought I had great hospital savvy now because I dressed very comfortably and I stopped wearing mascara so my tears wouldn't make black circles under my eyes. But now everyone back home was going to see me this way. Great. "How can I make it look like I haven't been crying? Help."

That evening I met Paul Murphy from Channel 4 in Utah. By this time the hospital had changed its policy and decided not to let any reporters or media cameras into the building. The security guard even came by every few hours to make sure we were protected. They knew I had agreed to this interview, so the security guards sneaked us down to the basement, and the cameraman filmed the interview in an empty classroom. I had written down many things I wanted to say, but during the interview I didn't refer to my paper. Paul let me focus on the things I wanted to say.

To me the real story through all of this illness is not the rarity of the disease, although I can understand people's curiosity. To me the real story is of community and faith. By this time, people from many different faiths in California were praying for David, as well as many people in Utah, English

Department colleagues and many others at BYU, our extended families, our neighbors, even my parents' neighbors' congregation on the other side of town. This was a great show of faith and very inspiring to be a part of. I talked about the possibility of a miracle and how I thought a miracle was going to happen, but I would accept the Lord's will if it didn't happen. I felt as if I could tell about my own spiritual feelings even in a medium that has no spiritual vocabulary. It was very satisfying. My interview aired that night on the 6:00 and 10:00 news.

The next morning I brought my daughters Cristie and Kathryn to the hospital so they could also talk to Paul Murphy, as he requested.

"Do we have to, Mom? This better be good, Mom."

"Are they going to ask us dumb questions, Mom, like 'How does it feel to have your father so sick.'"

"I really don't want to do this, Mom."

We took the camera crew to one of my favorite parks in Whittier, Penn Park, a place David and I had gone walking the day before our marriage. That day, eighteen years before, a news photographer happened to be in the park and took our picture for the newspaper.

Now, I walked with my teenage daughters, and we discussed the difficulty of David's sickness and the peace we received from all of the prayers people offered in our behalf. We got to thank the many people who wrote us and were pulling for us.

Later we watched the interviews on video tape, and we were glad we went out of our way to do them. One friend said to me later, "I saw you and your daughters on television. You are all so beautiful. It took me a while to be able to tell which one was the mom!"

"Oooooooo," I said. "Tell me that again."

Waiting and Waiting in the Waiting Room

Many times during the next few days I would arrive at the hospital in the morning, walk into David's room, and find his entire bed gone. Usually this meant he had been rolled down to the hyperbaric chamber, and he would be gone for several hours. Although I spent a lot of time by David's bed, I spent about the same amount of time sitting in the waiting room.

Situated outside the waiting room was the volunteers' desk. Usually during the day a hospital volunteer sat at the desk and helped people find their loved ones' beds. The volunteers also limited the number of people that could visit at one time. "Only two at a time, please." I got to know the volunteers because I, too, sat there day after day. We passed the time asking questions about each other's lives.

The Critical Care waiting room creates an unusual community. Most of the people in the room are the spouses, children, or close relatives of patients in Critical Care. Everyone is under enormous stress, because every person has a very sick friend or relative a few steps away in Critical Care. Families usually group together in the room, either on the same couch or around some of the tables. The television is constantly on, although eventually I found a way to turn down the sound. For some, mindless TV is the best coping tool. Mostly, though, people sit around and talk about their situations. As you see the same people there day after day, you start to share your story and they share theirs. Telling the story of sickness seems to be therapeutic for the waiting families.

After a while everyone gets to know everyone else, and families create bonds with other families in the room. My parents-in-law were extra friendly with other families, and we all got to know each person's background and what brought them to this stressful position.

One family was from Hacienda Heights, my parents' community. The father was in the hospital because of something to do with his eyes. The family was worried for him because he was an artist, and what would his life be like if he couldn't see? His wife was there every day with her grown children. She was very optimistic that he would pull through, and eventually he did. One day she brought me a small silver angel to pin to my shirt. "Angels will watch over us," the card said. I wore the angel so everyone could see.

Another woman was in the waiting room because her husband had had a heart attack. She became very friendly, especially with my parents-in-law. One day she brought funny-looking, tubelike bags made of striped terry cloth. "These bags are full of rice," she said. "You just need to heat them for a few seconds in a microwave, and then you have something warm to put on the back of your neck or anywhere it hurts." She brought bags to many of the families in the waiting room.

Sometimes when a grandmother or grandfather of a large family entered Critical Care, the entire family would converge on the waiting room. Those of us who were regulars would look at each other and roll our eyes as sometimes thirty adults and children filed in and took over the room for the night. These were the times I took off and went for walks or ate at the cafeteria. These large families would pull out cards for entertainment and would take every available chair, so there was no room for anyone else anyway. Since very few could actually go back to the room and see the sick relative, I first thought it was a waste to bring everyone. But then, as I considered it, I realized that there aren't that many large, strong families anymore, and that the unity these families showed was impressive.

Sometimes when it got too crowded I would sit out in the hall and talk or read. The large windows opened onto a courtyard with beautiful bare-trunked trees right outside the third-story window. Later we learned the trees were barkless eucalyptus, but for me and my children they took on personalities. Marissa thought they looked like elephant legs, and I always called them the elbow trees. We were in the middle of winter, and so there were not a lot of leaves, but since this was Southern California, not Utah, there was still green around. One day, Beth Cowles, my mother-in-law, noticed two hummingbirds nesting in one of the elbow crooks. The two birds built a nest the size of a golf ball. We checked on it every day.

Generally, people don't stay that long in Critical Care. Most recover enough to move to another floor. After a while, one older man and I noticed that nearly everyone who came into Critical Care the week after Christmas was gone now. Except our spouses. Every day we would check up on each other's families. Once I was escaping the crowded waiting room to stand in the quiet hall and stare at the elbow trees. This man passed by me and did a double take because I was crying. He came up to me.

"I've been watching you for a while now," he said. "You are really strong when you talk to your husband. But I know you hurt too because I see you crying in the hall afterwards. I can tell you have a lot of faith. I'm Catholic, and I know you are not, but I can tell we both pray to the same God."

"Thank you," I said.

He patted my back and left.

The three grown children of a very sick woman hung around the Critical Care waiting room for several days. They were quite sure their mother was not going to recover, since she was very sick and very old.

One day we passed them leaving as we were coming. "She died during the last hour," one of the brothers announced. "We have been here every minute, and the last hour we left to eat dinner. When we came back, we found out she died while we were gone."

We all felt awful, though we all knew no one was to blame.

As I sat down again in the familiar waiting room, I wondered how I would feel if David died while I was away.

. . .

While Delys, our families, and our friends waited impatiently for news, others waited nearly as anxiously. Delys had little time to call people because she was so busy at the hospital, so her friends had to be patient in waiting for news. Concerned hospital staff felt helpless waiting to see whether I would survive. At the BYU English Department, my illness was still the chief topic of conversation, and the mood in the halls remained somber while colleagues and students awaited news updates. At home, our five children could hardly think about anything else. They had trouble concentrating between phone calls and news reports about my condition. Later they described the twinges of irrational guilt they felt whenever they laughed or experienced momentary pleasure. Cristie, our oldest, took over as mother and tried to keep everyone occupied with videos and other distracting entertainment. Friends and colleagues wrote us daily to cheer our spirits and offer their prayerful support. The Baltes and Richan families wrote us a note or a card every single day.

And I waited, too, though I was the luckiest in many ways, for I waited without understanding what was happening to me and how my situation was affecting so many others.

Wake-up Call

By Saturday David had undergone major surgery and hyperbaric chamber treatments each day for five days in a row. During each surgery, the doctors would debride his wounds—take out the blackened or dead tissue. Every day the surgeons followed the path of the bacteria to find new areas of infection. By now the infection had covered his right arm, destroyed much of the flesh on his right side, crossed his abdomen and chest, and destroyed much of his left side. The doctors weren't certain where it would go next.

Necrotizing fasciitis destroys the fascia, or membrane surrounding the muscles, but it also destroys the layers of skin and fat above the fascia and sometimes the muscle under it. Then the toxins from the bacteria affect the whole system. This is why David's blood pressure was so low that he almost died.

Now he was on dopamine, which pulls the blood from all over the body to the heart so the blood pressure will be higher. David's condition was so desperate that the doctors were giving him five times the normal dosage. But this has unpleasant side effects. It deprives the extremities of blood, and often people lose toes and fingers because of this. The doctors decided to put leg cuffs on David to improve circulation to his toes. Several doctors seemed quite concerned that his toes, especially the big toes, had turned purple from lack of blood. In fact, many doctors walked into David's room and went right to his toes to see how they were doing. I just thought he had red and purple toe tips that would gradually fade into flesh color again. I didn't realize he was close to losing his toes because the tissue didn't have enough blood to keep it alive.

The leg cuffs covered each of David's legs. They squeezed his legs over and

70

over to encourage the blood flow. David hated the feel, and later when he was conscious, he had trouble sleeping with the constant leg squeezing.

Every time the doctors finished operating on David, they still just wrapped him in gauze and a sheet instead of stitching him back up. This way they could easily unwrap him the next day and be ready for more surgery. Besides, after the ravages of the bacteria, there was nothing to stitch. In the beginning the doctors changed David's bandages daily, and since he was mostly bandages, this took a long time.

The antibiotics, surgery, and hyperbaric chamber treatments seemed to be doing some good because the bacteria was not spreading nearly so fast now.

"But even if we rid his body of the bacteria, he will still be the sickest man in California," the doctors reminded me.

David was so critically ill that he always had a full-time nurse assigned just to him, and he kept his nurse on each shift busy. They were constantly opening pinched lines, replacing IV solutions, checking his blood pressure, and monitoring oxygen levels in his blood. One nurse looked unusually somber as she constantly shook her head in disbelief that David was still alive even after surviving five days. Her expression reminded me that he was still very sick.

Every day David was rolled away to the hyperbaric chamber, where the air was pumped full of 100-percent oxygen for forty-five minutes to an hour. He would return bright red from all that oxygen in his blood.

. . .

I think it unlikely that anyone who has never been there could comprehend what it feels like to be semiconscious in a strange place, unable to move or respond normally, surrounded by strangely dressed, masked, gloved medical personnel talking about you and your condition as if you weren't there to hear them. Probing, testing, evaluating. Twinges of pain, unpleasant pressures, insertions, exposures, violations.

I remember dimly a scene of operating room lights shining starkly onto covered tables, on one of which I was lying. I recall feeling cold. Even after multiple operations, my sense of suspense seeped up through the drug-induced stupor leading to the total brainlessness of anaesthetized unconsciousness, delaying for a small moment the inevitable blackout. My mind still conjures up images of green-gowned doctors selecting music to accompany their performance, closing in around me, joking among themselves and talking with businesslike voices about machines and procedures as if this were not me *in a life-threatening situation.*

As they came closer to actual surgery, my apprehension level tried to leap higher, but I felt trapped in a rapidly descending elevator, and no matter how high I jumped, I could only sink lower, lower, until everything faded into oblivion. I remember the last moments of semiconsciousness as if the fuzziness of peripheral vision were closing in, until what I could see and hear was reduced to a small circle immediately around me, and then fell in upon itself into blankness.

. . .

In his room between operations, David's arms were tied down so in his unconscious state he wouldn't pull out his IVs. As David started to regain consciousness, the nurse untied his arms for a while. But whenever David made a quick move with his arm to scratch his nose or something, the nurses jumped, thinking he might be pulling out the respirator.

The respirator prevented David from talking, which frustrated him, even in his semiconscious state. But as long as he was under so much morphine, the doctors kept him on the respirator, which did his breathing for him. I pulled up a chair close to his bed. Still, all that was left to touch was his left arm, and it was full of IVs. His thumb was constantly pinched by an oxygen monitor, and he had many tubes coming from his left arm. Nevertheless, I could hold his left hand and rub it and squeeze it, and I spent a lot of time doing that.

To communicate, David sometimes tried to write a word with his left hand, and sometimes he pointed to letters on an alphabet chart, but mostly he blinked and nodded. He was not fully conscious yet but slipped in and out of semiconsciousness. Sometimes I put his headphones on him and played some of his favorite tapes, and much of the time I just let him sleep.

The pharmacist, who we called Dr. John, brought in a large plastic bag of what looked like thick milk. "Here's dinner," he said laughing. The doctors were beginning to feed David intravenously. David's body was so depleted that he was almost starving, so he desperately needed nourishment.

At home, my parents, my children, and I discussed what we should do. David seemed to be kicking the disease, and we felt rather sure he would recover. By now, though, Christmas vacation was about over for the children, and school would start in a few days. Our two oldest were in high school, and if you miss more than a few days of high school, then you stress out the rest of the semester trying to catch up. Our friends in Utah offered to fly down and drive the children back home, but in the end, my parents decided to drive the minivan back to Utah and stay with the children until I came home.

On Monday my daughters pulled me aside. "All we have done this whole vacation is go to a funeral and the hospital," they observed. "Could we do one fun thing, Mom?" So I took both of them to a dress outlet, and we bought enough beautiful formals to last them the next year's worth of school dances. I tried on a few dresses myself, but I looked too much like a sturdy pioneer, so I gave it up for myself. Fortunately, everything was on a gigantic sale, and we felt we had a break from the oppression of the hospital.

The next day the children and my parents were all packed and ready to leave for Utah. We laid the formals carefully across the top of the suitcases so they wouldn't get smashed. I was hoping David would be alert enough to say good-bye to the children and know what he was doing. David had been in the hospital a whole week now. By Tuesday he was rather alert, so I brought all of the children back to his room. On the way in, we checked out the hummingbird nest in the elbow tree and noticed two tiny, jelly-bean-sized eggs. We stayed a short time, and David was alert enough to nod and blink at everyone.

On Wednesday morning I waved good-bye as my parents backed the van out of the driveway and then drove off with a very full car of five children, all throwing kisses from the backseats. I prayed they would be safe.

Within the day, the doctors removed David's respirator, and finally he was able to eat real food. I called the high school, middle school, and elementary school to tell them my children would miss some school and why, and please not to overwhelm them with questions and attention. It was too late, though, because all their friends and teachers had been following David's progress daily on the evening news.

Recalled to Life

One day I suddenly became fully conscious again. The week I spent in the near-death section of the Critical Care Unit blurs confusedly in my mind. My first really clear memory is the move to a new room in the regular Critical Care Unit. I remember thinking that it seemed strange to get promoted up to Critical Care. What did they call the place I had been before? The Really, Truly, Critically Critical Care Unit? What's worse than merely critical?

From this time on, even though I often drifted in and out of consciousness unpredictably, I remember things consecutively and more or less clearly. I celebrate that day as my return to personhood.

The new room was a vast improvement over the old one. For one thing, light beamed through the window and flooded the room from florescent fixtures in the ceiling. From my bed I couldn't see anything outside but a tiny piece of sky and the top corner of a building. Still, the light cheered me. Perhaps it was the influence of the morphine, but I remember basking in the brightness as if somehow I could actually feel it.

The new room seemed gigantic compared to the tiny cubicle I vaguely remembered inhabiting before. That room had barely contained me, my bed, what seemed like an entire pharmacy worth of IV bottles, cords, stands, and monitors, and the nurse who worked full-time keeping it all supplied and working properly. In the old room something was always beeping, signaling the nurse that an IV bag needed changing or that I required some injection. The new room, the largest in the unit, appeared wastefully spacious, and there were fewer things to make annoying noises.

One of my first official acts in my new environs was to check out the TV. I found I could receive local commercial stations, ESPN, and a special movie *channel. I'm somewhat embarrassed to recall that the TV remained on most of the time for several weeks. Though I wasn't coherent enough even to know what was playing at first, I found that in my diminished mental state (highly influenced by regular doses of morphine from one of the myriad IVs), whatever was on seemed much more interesting than I could have imagined. Even the commercials—which I normally detest and go to considerable lengths to avoid—fascinated me. Given the amount of brainpower I had to work with, it didn't take much to hold my attention.*

I soon learned why my room was so spacious. Later that afternoon, orderlies brought in three large tables, which they placed along the walls. Then for several hours various hospital personnel delivered a mountain of medical supplies: whole boxes of sterile gloves, masks, goggles, bandages of every size and description, cases of saline solution, sterile pads, scissors, tape, and machines and gadgets, the use of which I could only imagine.

I couldn't conceive what anyone could possibly do with so much stuff. But the more I thought about it that first day in the new room, the more ominous that medical mountain seemed. I found I couldn't keep my eyes off it. Even the TV commercials didn't distract me for long.

. . .

David was continuing to improve. Still, the doctors were cautious: "We're not out of the woods yet," they kept telling me. The bacteria was receding, the antibiotics were working, and David's body was successfully fighting off this strep A intruder. Now we had to worry about secondary infections and repairing his open body.

Denise from the hospital's public relations office asked me if I would come to another press conference about David. I said, "Sure, but one of these days I would like some notice so I can actually dress up and wear makeup so I don't look so hospital-dumpy." She put off the press conference until the next day.

Before this meeting with the media, I met Dr. Britto and Dr. Saketkhoo in the public relations office, and together we walked over to the press conference. The room was full of cameras and reporters. A few stations were missing because heavy rains had caused flooding and not everyone could make it to the hospital. Dr. Saketkhoo told how David had probably contracted the disease through a small cut in his finger. He talked about the hyperbaric chamber and the daily surgery and constant antibiotics. Dr. Britto told the press that David had lost about 50 percent of the skin from his torso. He mentioned that they planned to start covering him with skin grafts soon.

Then I answered questions about David. Reporters were worried about how contagious the disease was and would David get it again? "People have a better chance of winning the lottery than of contracting this disease. I'd go for the lottery, myself," I said. They asked about our family, his treatment, and what music he listened to in the hyperbaric chamber. Dr. Britto told me later he thought I would say the Mormon Tabernacle Choir or something. Instead, I said he was listening to U2, the Beatles, the Indigo Girls, and Lyle Lovett. There is a time for religious music, but the hyperbaric chamber is much more suited to other kinds.

Next I asked to make a statement. I said: "There is more to this story than just a scary disease. This is also a story of a community here in L.A. and in Utah coming together to pray for a very sick man. This is a story of goodness, and David's healing is a miracle. He had a 5-percent chance of living through the night initially, and now, a week later, his body is fighting off this disease.

"Los Angeles is known throughout the world as a city of riots, earthquakes, and fallen celebrities. But I love the Los Angeles area. I grew up here. I have seen the other side of L.A. David's sickness has brought out the goodness in people, and you can see it everywhere—from the hospital volunteers who helped my parents-in-law so much, to the doctors and nurses, to the members of our church who have brought food and donated blood, to many people we have never even met who have prayed for David. This is also a city of goodness. Remember, this is the City of Angels. I hope you not only tell the story of the scary flesh-eating bacteria but also the story of faith and miracles and the goodness of the people around here."

Afterward everyone wanted a photograph of David, but I didn't have one, so I drove to Hacienda Heights as quickly as I could in the rain. I grabbed one family picture from the wall and another we had just given to my parents for Christmas. I drove back to the hospital and stood around while everyone took pictures of the pictures.

One newspaper reporter pulled me aside. "I know you want the spiritual side of the story told. I've been in this business long enough to know that most of the other reporters won't tell that part of the story. But I am interested. Here is my card. Call me."

Later I called him, and he interviewed me and later David, and my brother and our church leaders in Hacienda Heights and in Provo. He boldly wrote headlines of "Man Saved by Miracle" in his articles, which ran over the next few days in a number of California papers.

. . .

The morning after my awakening I discovered what that frightening mountain of supplies was for.

I was tired before the ordeal even began. I was now meeting formally many of my team of doctors for the first time since regaining consciousness. One liked to make his rounds between midnight and 2:00 A.M., so he had awakened me, as he would most nights during my hospital stay. Not that I had been sleeping much anyway. As anyone who has been confined to a hospital bed for long knows, the noises and interruptions of hospital life prevent patients from getting much rest—even when sleep is aided by morphine. Outside my room, the Critical Care Unit desk kept up a steady barrage of noise. The section's computer printer—a noisy dot matrix—kept whining through the night. And of course the ubiquitous IV beepers went off whenever I ran out of something or the lines got twisted as I moved. At 6:00 A.M. I had been awakened, as I would be every day, for blood tests (often involving seven or eight separate vials for various interested parties) and X-rays.

About 7:45, while I was trying to summon enough energy and appetite to stomach my breakfast, two physical therapists, Stephanie and Rebecca, came into my room. They worked closely with me throughout my time in the hospital, and I came to love them both dearly. I referred to them as the Muses of Medicine. With Gina, another therapist, they became so expert and efficient, my father and I called them "The A Team."

Rebecca and Stephanie explained that though the bacteria had all been killed now, the toxins it had produced would continue to destroy tissue and muscle for several weeks at least. In addition, since much of my body had no skin to protect it, I was extremely susceptible to new infection. So, they explained, they would come in twice each day to debride me, which meant removing the new dead tissue and generally cleaning everything out. They euphemistically called this process "bandage changes."

"Okay," I said agreeably. That seemed reasonable and not too threatening.

Boy, was I wrong.

Thus began the most intensely painful ordeal of my life, to be repeated twice daily for between 2 and 2½ hours each time. Stephanie would come about fifteen minutes early for each debridement and bandage change to arrange the supplies and "butter" the bandages with an antiseptic ointment called Silvadene.

When Rebecca or another therapist arrived later, they, the nurses, and anyone else with the courage to stay donned gowns, masks, gloves, goggles, and hats. They weren't worried about catching the bacteria; that was all dead. They were afraid of infecting me with something one of them might be carrying.

The therapists would remove my bandages and painstakingly scrape off or spray saline solution at the dead tissue that had blackened since the last bandage change, cleaning everything carefully. The spray was less painful than the scraping, but both were almost unbearable. Then they would turn my stinging body to another angle and scrape and spray some more. Since the bacteria had affected all sides of my upper body, this was a long and tedious process. Though large areas of my body were numb from nerve damage, I could feel every move the therapists made to clean my wounds. It was by far the most intensely excruciating pain I have ever experienced or even imagined. Later the nurses offered me additional painkillers before the bandage changes, but the shots made me too nauseated to deal with the pain effectively, so I didn't use them often.

The cleaning process also involved painfully turning me from side to side, since the bacteria had affected areas all around my torso. We had to maneuver around all the tubes and wires still connected to my body. I had too little strength to turn myself, so the therapists and the attending nurse would struggle to help me move around to expose hard-to-reach areas. The pain and effort of moving added yet another layer of horror to the heap. Lying on my right side, where the damage was worst and where I had lost muscles in both side and arm, was itself agonizing. When all the debriding was finished, I had to attain verticality some-how—always with considerable help—so the therapists could rewrap bandages around my torso.

Nurses and therapists often encouraged me during the most intense moments. One particularly kind nurse, Teri, sometimes held my hand like a mother with a crying child. Delys did this when she was in town. My father's faithful presence—he almost never missed a bandage change—also helped. He and Delys became expert enough to advise weekend substitutes on procedures.

My mother, on the other hand, could not bear to watch. The scene was hor-rific, and my pain discouraged watchers. The therapists routinely sent away any visitors until after the bandage change—less for my sake than for theirs, because seeing my damaged body would sicken them. Stephanie told me later that she and the other therapists became nauseated themselves the first few times they saw me without my bandages. Sometimes they had to leave the room for a few moments. As they discussed my condition privately the first few days, they couldn't figure out how I could possibly even be alive. They saw almost no chance of my recovering enough to live anything like a normal life. My father-in-law, who bravely stayed through the ordeal on a number of occasions, said I looked like a cadaver with its head bantering wittily with the therapists and nurses.

Indeed, I constantly joked during these times to distract myself from the pain. That is how I have always dealt with difficult or painful situations, and these bandage changes called for more humor than anything else I had ever experienced. Stupid puns could get out of hand during especially harrowing moments. At the worst times I could only grit my teeth as tears streamed down my shaking face to keep from crying out in pain, which I was determined not to do. Sometimes, however, an unexpected pang would surprise me into a gasp or a brief "Whooah!" and I heard a deep, guttural grunting sound coming from somewhere inside my throat.

The agony of these daily debridements wore me out for the rest of the day, especially for the first few weeks. It had strong effects on the nurses and therapists who worked on me, too.

For example, remembering this time later, Stephanie wrote: "David is the most critical patient I have ever worked with. I had spoken with the plastic surgeon, but I was not prepared for the patient before me, who resembled an anatomy chart—so ill, so at risk. . . . I became encompassed by David. My family knew all about him and always asked, 'How's David today?'"

Another therapist, Joyce, wrote about first seeing me unbandaged: "I stood stunned by what I saw. The flesh was gone down to the muscle. I looked at David's face as he lay quietly looking off into the distance, amazed that this man was even alive. I had seen deep wounds before, but this was unbelievable. I knew that a miracle was needed if this man was to survive."

Anatomy Man

I was all alone staying at my parents' home now. Leon and Beth Cowles were staying at a home of some church members in Whittier. My parents were gone with the children, so I had to take care of things myself. David had been in the hospital for two weeks. I began every morning eating breakfast and taking care of business. I had to pay bills. I had to answer the phone, telling my brothers and sister and aunts and uncles and neighbors and church friends how we were doing. Everyone was very interested. I knew I could take the time to do this in the morning because my father-in-law arrived at the hospital early every day to feed David his breakfast. David couldn't bend his arms enough to feed himself.

I would get dressed, read through the wonderful daily packet of express mail from the English Department, then drive the twenty minutes to the hospital. I would stay and talk to David and leave when he needed to sleep. I would often eat lunch in the cafeteria, sometimes with my parents-in-law. In the evenings I would have to leave the hospital for a while for a bit of sanity, so I visited a different ethnic fast-food restaurant every night. I looked forward to this. And I started gaining weight because, although I was eating my normal amount, I was just sitting around a hospital all day with no exercise.

One day soon after the press conference, as I was sitting in the Critical Care waiting room, a woman came in the door and asked if I was Mrs. Cowles. She introduced herself as Fritzi, and said she had had this same necrotizing fasciitis David had. She had contracted it in January a few years earlier.

She brought pictures of her body before and after skin grafts, and she showed me her arm, which was fully recovered. She said that by October that same year, she was recovered enough to resume her job as a home nurse. She showed me pictures of her nurses and therapists and told stories of physical therapy and all of the work it took to get back the use of her arm. I was shocked by the graphic horror of the pictures, though her body had been ravaged far less than David's.

I took her back to David's room immediately so he could meet someone who had made it through all of this. They talked, and Fritzi gave us hope that we might have a somewhat normal life eventually.

When Fritzi left, I was resolved to see what David really looked like under all of the bandages. I felt I could take it. So when Rebecca and Stephanie started to prepare for the twice-daily bandage changes, I stepped in and said I wanted to see. Teri, the nurse, pulled me into the hall.

"Delys," she said seriously, "I suppose you need to face this sometime. But be warned, he is missing skin all over his body. It is very extensive. I've been a nurse in Critical Care for many years, but when I helped with David's first bandage change, I had to step out in the hall to make sure I wouldn't faint. The damage is that extensive. I can hardly believe that he is alive. If you need to leave during the bandage change, I will understand. Here, put on the mask, robe, hat, goggles, and gloves. We want to make sure he doesn't catch a secondary infection from us because his body is so open and vulnerable."

When we went back in, the bandages were off his arm, and I walked over to see how much was gone. I was expecting to see only bone, but to my surprise, there was a lot of muscle still on his arm. Of course, there was no skin or fat layer. Dr. Shin had told me his triceps were gone, but as I walked around his arm, I could see some triceps still there. I was excited and not faint at all. "Hey, there is still lots of muscle on this arm, David. Look at this. Here is your tricep—there is still some of it here!"

David looked like an illustration from an anatomy book. I could see all the muscles on his arm because there was no skin. As the therapists started working on his side, I could see right inside his body. The inner abdominal cavity was never cut, so I never saw his organs, but I could see his ribs, his hip bones, and down into his chest. His right side had no skin. His back flapped open from his shoulders to his hips ten inches deep. He had lost the fascia but not the skin layers on his back. His chest was wide open. His left side was not as extensively damaged, but it was missing a large strip of flesh one inch deep and about five to ten inches wide from under his arm to the bottom of his thigh. His neck had a large four-inch incision on each side and one in the middle, and all three just gaped open.

"I love you inside and out, David. And I know each well," I said.

The therapists "buttered" the gauze with Silvadene, an antibiotic ointment. They removed the old bandages, irrigated the area with a saline solution squirter, then suctioned up the extra water. This was excruciating for David. We often talked to David during this time to keep him distracted from the pain. Occasionally he would just blurt out a yell, but usually he handled the pain quietly. I helped him with Lamaze breathing and told him I would never hold it over him again that he had never been through labor. This was far worse than labor: it occurred twice a day, and there was no baby reward at the end.

I ended up helping with most of the afternoon bandage changes. I would hold up his arm for him and help turn his body over. I also served as the official photographer so the physical therapists could keep a visual record of his progress.

After the intense bandage changes, there was only one thing David could do: sleep.

. . .

The morphine often made it difficult for me to separate real life from the strange and surrealistic world of my dreams. Often while talking with someone, I would suddenly discover that my mind had wandered off onto its own paths for what could have been seconds or hours. Sometimes I would suddenly realize that someone was talking to me, and I would quickly blurt out something that had nothing whatever to do with what he or she was saying but made perfect sense in the lotos-world of my mind.

Only a few of my strange, drug-induced dreams remain in my waking memory, though small but powerful pieces of dream-memories still flash across my mind occasionally.

One day my mother entered my room while I was asleep. Not wanting to wake me, she sat quietly near my bed. She noticed that I was moving my lips in a very curious way. I apparently sensed her presence and awoke. She asked me what I had been dreaming about before the memory could escape. I answered, "I thought they were operating on my lips"—nearly the only part of my body the surgeons hadn't meddled with. The trauma of real life was reflected clearly in my unconsciousness.

Other dreams were equally unnerving. In one I saw myself as if my internal organs and circulatory system had been transformed into a video game on a screen, with Pac-Man bacteria racing through my body gobbling up everything in their path. In another, a collection of eccentric characters from Dickens novels moiled about in my mind shouting unintelligible things in Cockney accents and making threatening movements in my direction.

One night I lay for many hours in tortured and painful wakefulness because, as I told the nurses in the morning, I couldn't find the right unit of measurement to dream in. I remember trying the easy ones first: alphabetical arrangements, numerical ordering. Then I attempted to divide my consciousness up into little squares. I tried every categorical taxonomy I could imagine, logical and illogical, but I couldn't find one that would fit whatever dream-matter seemed waiting for the proper container. I finally fell asleep in complete frustration and utter exhaustion.

In the meantime, my daily visits to the hyperbaric chamber increased my exhaustion and frustration. For one thing, the two-hour sessions nearly bored me to death. Myriad wires and tubes still sprouted from various parts of my battered body. Inside the belly of the hyperbaric monster, I had to lie very still to keep from messing up these attachments. Generally the staff played music through speakers in the chamber, and that came as close as anything could to entertaining me. Outside the window next to my head was a tiny television, but the sound didn't work, and I didn't have the mental alertness to watch without hearing.

Boredom wasn't the worst part of the hyperbaric chamber, however. Though I had never been claustrophobic before, I found myself feeling increasingly panicked at the close quarters as the sessions went on. My ever-present nausea also increased until I avoided vomiting only with the greatest difficulty. The doctors gave me antianxiety medications, which helped some. But each day as the time for my hyperbaric sessions approached, I could only anticipate the ordeal with genuine horror.

After several weeks, I spoke to Dr. Saketkhoo about my aversion to the chamber. I told him that with a hyperbaric session and two lengthy and painful bandage changes each day, I had little time and less energy left for the business of regaining strength, dexterity, and motor skills. One day he told me that though hyperbaric therapy was still helping, it was no longer as essential as it had been earlier. He said I could choose whether to continue with it or not. I chose not, to my great and lasting relief. Though I recognize the importance of the hyperbaric chamber in my survival and recovery, and though I will always be grateful to those who worked so diligently to make that therapy work for me, I sincerely hope I never see the inside of one of those infernal machines again.

. . .

The hospital staff, including the nutritionist, were beginning to worry about a new problem. David was so nauseous that he could hardly eat anything. The doctors had removed the respirator, so David was theoretically able to eat by mouth, not just by IV. He started with small bites of soft foods, and then he moved up to the actual meals. Even the thought of food, though, made him sick. He could drink fruit juice, and I could talk him into a few bites of something soft such as applesauce or potatoes, but forget anything else.

His father came in every morning and fed David breakfast, then helped with the morning bandage change. David ate more at breakfast than at any other time. Then later I came in and spent time with him; then his mother and father would return in the afternoon. David's parents and I sometimes ate dinner together at the cafeteria, and we shared concerns about David. The dream about the lips kept us laughing for a long time.

The nurses and I tried to feed David, but nothing worked. He always mentioned the strong nausea that took away his appetite and often caused him to throw up what small amounts he could eat.

Eventually the doctor said, "David absolutely needs to eat more. He is starving to death. His calorie requirements are enormous now as his body is repairing extensive damage. He needs about 6,000 calories a day."

"Six thousand calories a day!" I replied. "Why can't someone require me to eat 6,000 calories. I think I could pull it off."

But David couldn't. The hospital nutritionist tried all kinds of fattening foods. Every few hours the kitchen sent a can of Ensure, a high-calorie drink. But nothing took away David's appetite like a can of Ensure. He sent all the cans back, usually unopened.

One afternoon I drove to a local health-food store to ask some advice. I explained my husband's problem, and I asked if they had any acidophilus to help his nausea. The man said we could try the yogurt with acidophilus, but David's antibiotic dose was so high that the medicine would quickly destroy the good bacteria from the acidophilus. It wouldn't really have time to work. I got some yogurt anyway, and took it back to David. He took only a few bites.

After a few days of starving, David was put back on nutrition by IV.

. . .

On one occasion, after the most serious danger was over and I had spoken coherently with Delys and the doctors, something unexpected happened. I remember Dr. Saketkhoo becoming panicked, but my consciousness was receding too quickly for me to understand what was happening. Nurses and doctors surrounded me with worried voices. My body could sense but not feel them doing things to it—prodding, inserting, trying one thing and then another.

A few minutes later—how long I couldn't have said—my consciousness suddenly emerged from nothing into a dreamlike state. I sensed the crowd of people in the room and heard muffled voices, then gradually achieved relative clarity. Suddenly I realized I was being moved. I remember trying to say something, to ask what was happening and why they were taking me away. Delys and Dr. Saketkhoo were there. Someone explained that I had blacked out unexpectedly as the nurse was removing a chest catheter, and I nearly died once again. They were rushing me to the hyperbaric chamber to remove the possibility of any air bubbles in my blood.

"Please, don't take me back there," I begged. I couldn't stand the thought of spending two hours in the claustrophobic closeness of that horrible tube.

Delys leaned over me and tried to explain how important it was that I endure the chamber again, but in my present condition I could feel only total despair.

"I'm really sorry," I recall pleading piteously. "I must have made a mistake. Please don't make me go there now. I promise I won't do it again."

The last thing I remember is Delys's face disappearing behind me as the orderlies pushed my bed through the door and into the hall.

I survived the chamber, and the danger passed.

The Miracle Man

Seemingly from the moment I regained consciousness, everyone around me wanted to talk about my remarkable survival. I have never heard the word miracle used so often or so freely by so many people. I can't begin to count the number of hospital personnel— from doctors and nurses to cleaners and orderlies—who came into my room to see "the Miracle Man." It quickly became apparent to me that for whatever reason, my life had been spared in a highly unusual way.

I soon found out part of how that came about. I learned of the prayers and good wishes of literally thousands of people—friends, colleagues, hospital personnel, and people who heard of my plight through the news media. I was touched to learn that my nurses and therapists and their families were praying for me. Throughout my time in the hospital, it seemed that nearly everyone who heard about my case had contributed to the powerful outpouring of love and faith on my behalf.

Even before I regained consciousness, the hospital was getting so many phone calls from Utah and throughout the country inquiring about my condition that the public relations department called Joyce Baggerly, the English Department's amazing secretary, for help. The department was experiencing similar problems, as literally hundreds of calls came in from concerned people seeking information about my condition. Joyce wisely converted the department phone number into what came to be called the "David Cowles Hot Line." Joyce left phone-mail messages providing updates, changed three times daily for the first week, including the weekend. For more than a month she added daily reports on my condition.

Literally hundreds of people called the hot line for the most up-to-date information available. Relatives and concerned friends in California also learned to check there. We sometimes joked that I even called in occasionally to find out *how I was doing that day.*

Support came in other ways as well: cards and letters, faxes, books, gifts, kind wishes from everywhere.

The English Department was especially supportive. At 3:00 every afternoon the department express-mailed me a box or large envelope with messages from colleagues and students. As Joyce put it in the department's history:

> The envelope contains many different forms of love. Faxes have come from all over the United States, students have drawn booklets of their favorite subjects taught by David, extraordinary messages left on phone mail are put on ordinary phone message slips, books of cartoons (so far, 3 editions of Calvin & Hobbes), and several CDs and cassette tapes. Some faculty members come every morning to put their daily greetings in the envelope before they go to their offices: notes, letters, epistles, allegories, puns, jokes, or hand-drawn cartoons; one even puts in a copy of the university newspaper.

These offerings, along with greetings from friends and others, were the high point of each day in the hospital. Many of my colleagues and friends sent heartfelt letters that moved me deeply and helped sustain me through the most difficult times.

One of the most enjoyable missives from a colleague included a delightful list I can't resist including in its entirety:

The Top Ten Reasons
for Contracting Streptococcus A
during the Christmas Holidays

10. The resulting ICU hospitalization guarantees you will not feel alone during the holidays.

9. It provides needed seasonal employment for doctors, nurses, and technicians.

8. The hyperbaric chamber gives you new insight into high-pressure situations.

7. It allows you to miss the all-important Mid-Year Department Conference without feeling guilty.

6. It also gives you a chance to miss out on the interminable but fascinating University Self-Study reports and meetings.

5. You don't have to shovel any snow for a while.

4. It's a surefire way to lose the extra pounds that have accumulated since Thanksgiving.

3. It's a convenient and irrefutable excuse for missing holiday in-law gatherings.

2. The expression "What's eating you?" will no longer be a mere cliché.

1. Besides giving you your fifteen minutes of fame, it places you in the thoughts, hearts, and prayers of those who know you.

Doctors, nurses, and other hospital personnel from many religious denominations stopped by my room to assure me they were praying on my behalf. Some of my physical therapists told me their Bible study group had begun praying for me regularly. I received letters from people throughout the United States that tell of fervent prayers for my recovery. My colleagues reported being approached by complete strangers at academic conferences far from Utah, who asked how I was doing. Many of these were professors who had seen my story on news broadcasts by stations that thought my illness newsworthy but which made no mention of my later recovery—the real story, as far as I am concerned. Long-lost friends called to tell me of entire congregations praying for me in Oregon, New York, Washington, Arizona. I received calls of concern from friends in England and elsewhere. Many of these people experienced their own personal spiritual moments.

My survival and recovery was obviously the result of many prayers of faith offered by people with vastly different religious backgrounds. One day early in my recovery a friendly nurse was discussing with me the miraculous nature of my survival. During the conversation she mentioned that she was a devout Jehovah's Witness. Apparently accustomed to negative reactions to that fact, she blushed and stammered, "I guess we're the enemy, aren't we." To me at that time this idea seemed preposterous. "You're not the enemy," I remember murmuring through my narcotic haze. "Satan is the enemy. Evil is the enemy. Death and suffering are the enemy. Surely we're on the same side."

That fact is one of the obvious lessons of my experience. The faith to cause miracles is not the exclusive province of any particular denomination or belief. And the love and kindness behind the miracle-making prayers of faith do not stop to question someone's religious or political affiliation. Love, as the apostle Paul writes, is no respecter of persons. It just is.

Many people, from Utah and elsewhere, also contributed more concretely, by donating to a trust fund set up by Delys's brother Brent to help us with expenses. Periodically, I received door-sized sheets of paper that had been posted outside my office, filled with notes of care and concern from students, faculty, and friends. Local members of our church in California found a place for my parents to stay and donated so much blood the hospital had much more than they needed for my operations and occasional transfusions. Members of our church around the nation held special fasts and offered prayers in my behalf. A Roman Catholic colleague sent me a note informing me that a special mass would be held for me.

It became obvious to me that my survival and eventual recovery owed much to all these caring people, and I was astounded by the sustaining love and support offered so generously.

One morning after I had somehow survived a particularly horrendous day of crisis, Joyce Baggerly talked with the head nurse of the Critical Care Unit to get information for the daily update. The nurse told her that it was yet another miracle day: "And I know you people believe in miracles," she said. "In fact, I would say that you people in Utah have kept this man alive with your prayers, because he should be dead with what he's had."

One of my favorite testimonials to the spiritual powers at work in my survival came from the hospital's head pharmacist, a moustached comic named John Ziesler. He was known universally as Dr. John, perhaps because of his difficult surname, or perhaps because of his informal and delightfully humorous personality. He always wore a white lab coat with "Dr. John" embroidered on the chest as if it were a mechanic's uniform. Only his ties—always colorful and ranging from wild stripes to Bugs Bunny cartoon characters—seemed to change.

Dr. John seemed always to be trailing a group of interns from Denmark or China or some other equally exotic place. And for some reason I never quite understood, they were always very beautiful young women—though he swore that was strictly coincidental.

Dr. John would always bring new interns to visit me to see what he called the most remarkable case he had ever worked with. And he stopped by my room each day to check up on me and to tell me whatever stupid jokes he had heard on a radio station while driving to work that morning.

89

He played an integral part in my treatment. He determined how I would receive drugs and nourishment throughout my time in the hospital. He also helped with my occasional bouts with secondary infections and with my perpetual struggles with nausea. Dr. John's innovative treatments made a substantial difference in my survival and eventual recovery. And his concern, good humor, and friendship made the long weeks of rehabilitation much less bleak than they otherwise would have been.

Early on I took the opportunity to thank Dr. John for his concern and hard work on my behalf. He smiled and pointed toward the ceiling. "Don't thank me," he said. "Thank Him. I was clearly directed every step of the way. Every time I had to make a decision, the right answer just sort of appeared in my mind, and I knew it would be the right choice. And it always was. I'm pretty sure the other doctors had similar help, though they might not admit where it came from."

"Does this happen often?" I asked.

"Not to me," Dr. John said. "I'm not particularly religious or anything. But you're obviously getting special help for some reason."

I smiled. "Lots of people have been praying pretty hard for me."

"It's working," he said.

Can You Move Your Fingers?

My parents had made the trip to Utah safely with all of the children. But a few days before they even left California, I got a call from Beth.

"I hate to even tell you this, Delys, but I've got some bad news. Yesterday the Fullers were eating breakfast, and they looked out the back window to see your roof had turned into a river of ice. They called me, and we got the spare key and looked inside. You know the water pipe in your ceiling going to the swamp cooler? Well, the temperatures here have been below zero. That pipe froze and broke, spraying water all over your roof. Much of this water has flooded your front room."

"Oh, no. What happened to the piano?"

"The bad news is that water poured down onto your grand piano and then to the floor. The carpet, ceiling, and walls are ruined."

"Is there any good news?"

"The good news is that the lid on the grand was open, so the water just ran down the slanted lid to the floor. The piano doesn't seem to be damaged."

"Wow." I was relieved. I didn't care that much about the carpets and ceilings. They are easily replaced. But our 7' 9" Yamaha Grand Piano was the only piece of furniture we owned that was worth anything at all. Six years ago we bought the piano with all of the money we had and with a loan from the credit union. We are still paying it off. But back then we decided that music was so important to us that it was worth it to drive very old cars in order to have a wonderful piano. The bass notes are so rich that I love to walk by the piano and just play low D. The piano is a center of our lives: all our children have taken piano lessons, David and I play a lot, and

91

I have taught piano lessons for many years. The piano was not damaged! Let's hear it for polyurethane finishes.

"I'll bet you feel like Job now, Delys."

"Oh, no," I replied. "Not unless I lose your friendship. Job lost his friends, and we still have ours."

And in the next few days our friends really pulled through.

David Fuller and Beth immediately moved the piano and dried the lid. They moved anything else of value that could get soaked, such as our rare books. We usually leave the piano lid down, but David recorded some of his compositions on tape right before Christmas vacation, and the lid was fortunately left up after the recordings. They turned off the water to the house to stop the water flow.

When news of the flooded house spread, neighbors and church members were so relieved to be doing something to help us besides pray and write letters that many showed up to help. LeeAnn Powell, the president of our church's women's group, organized church members in the cleanup. They moved our belongings out of the living room, put buckets around to catch the water, pulled up the carpets, and rounded up some fans. I tried not to think about the mess we had left behind in a hurry when we rushed away for vacation.

As it came time for my parents to arrive with my children, Paul Hedengren found the source of the flooding problem and turned the swamp cooler water pipe off so he could turn the rest of the house water on. People rushed to get our house ready for my family to arrive. Friends moved furniture, vacuumed, cleaned, and piled the clutter. Some stripped the beds and washed the sheets before my family arrived. Other friends worked on the pipes in the swamp cooler area so they could fix the plumbing. By the time my parents arrived, my fellow church members had made my home much more liveable.

On the day my parents drove my children from California to Utah (a twelve-hour drive), members of my church had a meal ready to deliver anytime they arrived. Beth was the scout, and when the van drove into the garage, she made a phone call, and my church friends brought over a wonderful meal. During this time while I was far away, my friends showered my parents and children with food, attention, snow removal service, and offers to babysit the little ones.

At home, my parents heaped attention on the children to help them feel loved and secure. They walked Steven to school, and they got on the floor and colored with Marissa. They drove Cristie and Kathryn to high school, and Robby to his piano lessons. They spent time talking to each child, and they spent hours answering our phone and passing on information.

One day the Dean of the College of Humanities at Brigham Young University and his wife stopped by the hospital, since they were in California visiting a daughter. He told me the university would cover David's classes that coming winter semester, and they would cover my classes for as long as I needed to be in California. I thanked him for his generosity and took him up on the offer. I knew David was beginning to recover, and I wanted to be with him as long as I could. I knew my children were going through stressful times, and they needed me too. I also knew that people could substitute for a while at the beginning of a semester, but not for too long. I talked to David, and I decided to stay through January 18, miss four days of teaching, then fly home and be with the children. I would then fly back every weekend I could to be with David. David's parents returned to Portland to take down their Christmas decorations and resolve some affairs. They planned to fly back to California the day after I left.

By now the surgeons had fully debrided David's arm and had placed skin grafts on his forearm. He continued to have many surgeries, but now they were to replace skin, not to remove it. His thighs became the donor spots, and Dr. Britto, the plastic surgeon, said they could "harvest" skin from the same site every two weeks. They took something like a cheese slicer, sliced a thin layer of skin about six inches long, poked holes in it, and then stretched it until it was several times larger. This way they could cover him with skin faster. They stapled the skin on, covered everything with bandages, and told David not to move for a week. The skin grafts looked bumpy like chicken skin. Surprisingly, the donor sites, bright red and black with clotted blood, hurt far more than the places that were receiving grafts.

David's skin grafts on his arm "took" well. Dr. Britto removed the bandages from the forearm after ten days. He looked at the blackened arm and pronounced the skin as mostly healthy. I looked at the black-and-red arm wondering if anything looked different with skin on. I couldn't see any change. It looked awful. Now they kept David's right arm and hand in a metal brace to try to straighten it and force the muscles to stretch and not just contract. He had to wear it twenty-four hours a day for months. David hated the brace.

Dr. Britto talked to me privately about David's arm. He told me they had decided to leave his arm because it had enough live tissue to keep it healthy. But he told me that the arm would probably be completely lame. They didn't expect him to be able to use it at all. Maybe, if they were lucky, he would be able to sign his name with his right hand, but that would probably be all.

Dr. Shin told me they had to cut a lot of dead tissue around the central nerve going down his arm. They did all they could to keep the nerve intact and alive, but they did not have much hope about his hand functioning fully. Once when they were scraping around the nerve, Dr. Shin had nicked it. He was afraid the nerve was damaged and that David would not be able to move his fingers at all.

David did not know the extent of the damage in his arm. He didn't even know the doctors were considering amputation. Now that he was fully conscious (except for regular lapses in concentration), I began to tell him all of the details of what happened to him over the last several weeks, including the problems with his arm.

. . .

People continued to come in and check my toes to see if they were still purple, but my toes seemed to please most everyone who came by. Now the focus was on my arm. Dr. Shin and Dr. Britto came in every day to check on my skin grafts and wounds. One day Dr. Shin was particularly interested in my right arm.

"Okay," Dr. Shin said. "Now for the important question. Can you move your fingers at all?"

"Sure," I said, wiggling them as much as my hated arm-and-hand brace would allow. "No problem."

Dr. Shin's sudden silence surprised me. He seemed amazed and moved. "You've made my day," he said. His voice seemed to shake slightly. "In fact, you've made my entire week."

"I'm pleased," I said. "Why?"

When he spoke again, his voice was softer. "I was sure we'd cut the nerve to your hand when we were cleaning out some of the dead tissue. We actually had to pick the nerve up, like a string, and scrape off the dead parts. We were almost certain you'd lose the use of your hand."

I was shocked. How could I have lived without my hand. I thought of all the things I used it for. I typed endlessly on my computer keyboard. I kept my sanity by playing and composing on the piano. I knew by now how hard it was to eat and write left-handed. And tennis would have been impossible.

Later, when I told Delys about this conversation, she paused, and then shocked me again. "It was much worse than that," she said. "Three times in those first days the surgical team included someone prepared to amputate your right arm. They strongly disagreed about whether or not to do it. Some thought they could only save your life by quickly cutting past where the bacteria was to prevent it spreading elsewhere and to stop it from making toxins. I told them you played the piano and to do everything possible to save the arm. They kept deciding to wait until the next day before amputating, but they offered little hope for saving the arm at all, much less for it having normal function."

"Miracle number one, my life. Miracle number two, my arm stays. Miracle number three, I can move my fingers."

I thought hard about what life would have been like without my right arm. Delys wondered whether I would have preferred death to life without my arm. I knew that was a weak thought, but I suspected it was true.

I still wondered whether I'd ever be able to play the piano again—the single most important reason I cared about my hand. I remember wondering whether I could buy a synthesizer with a sequencer so I could continue to compose and record my pieces a little at a time with just my left hand.

Pondering

Lying in my hospital bed alone for many hours with only commercial television to entertain me (I still could not hold a book up long enough to read more than a page), I had lots and lots of time to think. In my previous life (abbreviated B.S. for Before Streptococcus), I had often lamented how little time I had to ponder things that really mattered. Though this was not quite what I had in mind, I did do a great deal of thinking.

For one thing, surviving something as serious as flesh-eating bacteria demands some very serious and philosophical thinking. Coming as close to death as I did made me look closely at my life and ask myself some very difficult questions. If my life had suddenly ended shortly after Christmas 1994, what would it all have meant? What things really mattered, and what didn't?

First, my brush with death did not really scare me. I found that I am not afraid to die. In fact, in some ways I look forward to it. I don't have a death wish or anything like that. But two very significant personal experiences have convinced me that life continues beyond our earthly deaths, and that that life is immensely desirable. These are very personal and even sacred experiences to me, and I hesitate to share them. But at least parts of both seem necessary to understanding my experience.

The first occurred in May 1993. While working as a missionary in Venezuela in the mid-1970s, I became very close to a Spanish family living there. José and Carmen Aguilar and their daughter, Eva (remember her from the Vernal experience in the Prologue) became my very close friends. They came to consider me a sort of adopted member of their family, and I felt as if José and Carmen were my second parents and Eva the sister I never had. Several years after my return to the United States, the Aguilars moved to the

Los Angeles area, several blocks from Delys's parents' home in Hacienda Heights. Over the years we remained very close.

In 1988 and 1991, José survived leukemia twice—each time the only patient in the hospital ward to eventually walk out. That story involves miraculous healings similar to my own (though Eva jokingly insists he was just too stubborn to go until he was good and ready). Still, everyone assumed that given his health problems, José would be the first to die.

Suddenly, however, Carmen—always healthy and upbeat—fell seriously ill. She was hospitalized with advanced cancer. When Eva told me over the phone, I was shocked. We all hoped and prayed Carmen would quickly recover.

Two nights later, at about 5:00 A.M., while I slept soundly, my dreams were interrupted by one of the most powerful and vivid visions I have ever experienced. It was unlike any dream I have ever had in its realism and its emotional impact. I saw and heard Carmen Aguilar as clearly as if she stood next to me. She told me her body had just died and that her spirit was moving into something joyous and peaceful and wonderful. She emanated a powerful spirit of love and happiness that I will never forget. Carmen quickly communicated to me several pieces of information and some explicit instructions regarding her family. Then she took her leave, and I awoke feeling calm and happy for Carmen.

The following morning I called Eva as early as I dared. Before I could say anything, she told me her mother had died during the night—minutes before my "dream." Though obviously suffering from the loss, Eva felt comforted because her mother had also visited her, at almost exactly the same time she had come to me. Carmen had told Eva she was blissfully happy, free from pain for the first time in years, and just embarking on an exciting and beautiful journey. I told Eva what I had experienced, and we both wept with joy. We discovered later that Carmen had also visited José at the same time, with expressions of love and hope for him as well.

The powerful feelings that accompanied these "visions" have remained with all three of us. None of us fears death. We all look forward to experiencing what we felt from Carmen the night she died.

The second incident is even more personal—and even more sacred to me. Several years ago I experienced perhaps the most memorable and significant event of my life—even eclipsing my illness and its aftermath. Because of certain needs involving myself and others, I was blessed with what I can only call a minor vision of the life beyond this one. I felt I perceived a small corner of that

97

world—certainly not with the kind of detail and clarity some other people describe. The details I did sense I do not feel comfortable sharing except on rare occasions. But the sense of that moment and the feelings that accompanied it will never dim from my mind and spirit.

For me, this world is like a terrarium with its own environment and ecosystem. The world beyond is not like ours, and far exceeds our ability to comprehend. But I believe as strongly as anything in my life that it exists, and that it is the most beautiful and joyous state imaginable, and far more. Though I love my life here, I want more than anything else to get there, and to experience again what I just began to perceive in the vision.

So when the time comes, I am not afraid to die.

In the interminable hours I spent alone in the hospital bed—unable even to hold a book up to read—I found serenity. I didn't know why I had been stricken with this devastating disease, much less why God had worked miracles to keep me alive. But I knew He had His reasons for both. When the time came, I knew I would go to Him willingly and joyfully. But if I was going to remain on earth a while longer, I would do everything I could to serve him and to bless his children. And right now that meant recovering as quickly and as fully as possible.

I determined that if a little pain or a bit more effort would take even a few minutes off my total recovery time, it was well worth it.

. . .

I tried to keep David entertained to keep his mind occupied. He tried to read, but his mind was not focused enough to read, and he had too little strength even to turn a page. I requested a VCR in his room, and the nurses kindly obliged, although VCRs are rarely used in the Critical Care Unit. I got a list of suggested videos from nurses and doctors and set out down Whittier Boulevard looking for a video store. I came across a Blockbuster Video. Inside, I approached the clerk and told him I wasn't a permanent resident, but I wanted to check out films for my husband in the Critical Care Unit at Presbyterian Intercommunity Hospital. I told him I had been on TV on the news a lot the night before. He said he recognized me, but I knew he didn't. He let me check out some videos anyway.

As I was standing in line to pay for the movies, I noticed the music playing over the store's sound system. Long before I was conscious of listening, the words floated around in my brain, and I realized that I was listening to "The Impossible Dream." I stared at the speaker on the ceiling and started to cry.

"This is a song about my husband," I told the clerk. "Listen to the words." We listened to the end of the song.

"Thank you for playing this music. It is about my life right now."

I left quickly, before another song came on, and I sat in the car and wept.

Crying

Despite the phenomenal speed of my recovery, I wasn't satisfied. In fact, the faster I progressed, the more I craved full and complete recovery NOW. TODAY.

Three weeks into my hospital stay, when Rebecca and Stephanie remarked again on the astounding progress I had made, I lost it. Uncontrollable tears slid down my cheeks, embarrassing me horribly. But I couldn't stop them.

"I know how well I'm doing," I said, my voice shaky with emotional vibrato. "I know I shouldn't even be alive, let alone in possession of all my body parts. But I really, really like my life. And I want it back."

In general, I suppose I held up remarkably well. But throughout my time in the hospital and for several months after my escape from it, my emotions remained very close to the surface. Intellectually, of course, I reject the macho idea that a man should never cry. In actual practice, however, the irrational ideals of maleness cultured into me simply by my growing up in the America of the late 1950s and 1960s have proven hard to shake.

I knew this from several past experiences. For example, during several of my years of doctoral study at the University of Chicago in the early 1980s, Delys worked to support the family while I concentrated on passing my qualifying exams and finishing my dissertation. Obviously this arrangement made perfect sense: the sooner I could finish my degree, the sooner we could find a real job (or as close to that as academics allows) and Delys could begin her own graduate work and spend more time with the children. But recognizing the practical sense of this arrangement didn't keep me from feeling irrational guilt that I was not the one supporting my family. "Hey," the voice in my head kept whispering, "Donna Reed never had to work to support her family." Neither did Beaver

Cleaver's mom, or Laura Petrie, or any of the other TV mothers who had helped shape my consciousness.

So though my head told me it was okay for a man to cry, even in front of other people, part of me was stubbornly embarrassed at any outward show of emotions. And the worst of it now was that those emotions were prone to take over without warning and often at the most inconvenient times.

For instance, one day a prominent leader from my church who had just spoken at a series of meetings in the area dropped in to see me. We had never met, but he had heard of my plight and wanted to offer comfort and encouragement. He also gave me a healing spiritual blessing. Then he told me that all the leading councils of my church were including me in their prayers. That news immediately launched me into an emotional mode. I couldn't stop the tears.

This man understood, I think, better than I did that a continuing ordeal like mine generates a great deal of emotion. Those feelings eventually require venting. And it seemed that my vents were constantly opening. I would suddenly burst into tears when I thought of family or friends, my work as a teacher, my dramatic and seemingly miraculous survival, the hospital staff, the natural beauty of the outside world I could not see from my bed, or almost anything else. Occasionally, though not often, I cried at what I had lost through my illness and at the prospect of a long and painful rehabilitation. I even cried about the characters in my unfinished novel. Sometimes I cried for no apparent reason. That would confuse me, which made me want to cry even more.

Delys had placed a picture of my family near my bed where I could easily see it. I spent hours staring at the photograph, missing each of my children individually and all of them collectively. I cried until my tear ducts, apparently empty from overuse, refused to produce more tears. Surprisingly, the one thing I didn't cry about was the pain.

I had the same problem whenever I received visitors or phone calls from people I had known before my illness. Several friends from Provo dropped in while in the L.A. area, and colleagues, friends, and neighbors bombarded me with letters and calls. Every one seemed like a hand reaching into my chest (which wouldn't have been difficult, since much of my torso still gaped open under the bandages), grabbing my heart, and pulling it out where everybody could see it. I am a rather private person, and I have always felt a bit vulnerable exposing myself too much. (Writing this book is very difficult for me for that reason.)

One night I had a nightmarish vision in which a group of my colleagues and

101

former students stood around my bed analyzing my battered body and soul as if I were a literary text. "How would you describe the dominant theme of this work?" one senior professor asked. "I'm not sure," said a student in the group, "but he sure cries a lot, doesn't he?"

. . .

I knew my time in California was ending quickly. I began to wrap up projects and set David up so he could get along without me. We arranged to have a telephone plugged in his room so I could call him every day. I ate at the last of the ethnic fast-food places near the hospital.

A few days before I left, I got brave and decided to face the financial end of this sickness. I wandered around the main floor until I found the billing department. Inside, I spoke to one of the financial counselors and asked her if I could find out the total so far for my husband's stay. She pulled it up on the computer and told me that his bill was for $140,000. At that time he had been in the hospital ten days. It didn't take much arithmetic to figure out that it was costing him $14,000 a day. Now this was only for the hospital. I knew he had ten doctors at any given time, and they each charged for the operations and the daily visits.

I tried hard to be emotionally tough, but this was so much money that I immediately started crying.

"Does this include the physical therapists? They spend five hours a day with him."

"Yes."

"Does this include the hyperbaric chamber? He has spent hours in that chamber."

She didn't know, made a call, and then told me, "No. They bill separately."

"Does this include any of the doctors?"

"No."

"Oh my. I believe we will be making payments to your hospital for the rest of our lives."

She checked out our insurance and told me what I already knew: we owed $4,000 plus 2 percent of everything after $4,000. And they would pay nothing after $1,000,000. I figured it would only be a matter of a few months and we would be past the $1,000,000 mark. Then David wouldn't have insurance from our company for the rest of his life, and we would surely be bankrupt. I looked at the computer screen for an itemized segment of the bill and was amazed at the detail: every pill, every shot, every blood test, every X-ray was listed and charged.

I apologized for crying so uncontrollably but said I had sticker shock. I asked her what I should do with such an enormous bill. She gave me pamphlets on social security benefits. She also looked up our company in a large notebook and told me that they have an agreement with the hospital that the hospital will discount the bill for the insurance company.

I wandered around the hospital alone for a long time. I stared out windows, looked at the elbow trees, and hung around empty hallways.

Later I returned, red-eyed, to David's room. He still couldn't eat because of nausea. I looked at the full dinner they brought him and wondered how much the meals cost in Critical Care. I joked that they probably charged $50 a day for meals. From that day on, with the nurses' permission, I ate whatever was left of David's dinner. We were going to get our money's worth!

Saying Good-bye

David had entered the hospital on December 27, and now it was January 17, three weeks later. He was obviously going to live: the bacteria had been gone for two weeks, the first of the skin grafts had taken, and he was able to sit up for a few seconds—with a lot of help. He still could not eat well because of the nausea, and he had had to fight off a secondary bacterial infection called pseudomonas, which is common in people who have open wounds like David's.

But now the secondary infection was gone, and he continued to improve. I felt it was time I could return to Provo and take care of my job and our children. David would not be alone. Beth and Leon, his parents, would fly back the day after I left, and my parents and Eva and Danny Thron could come and keep him company too.

On the way to the airport, I stopped by the hospital to rub his hand and say good-bye. I couldn't kiss him because I didn't want to risk infecting him. Besides, I couldn't even reach his face in the middle of the bed. Several news stations called the hospital and wanted to be at the airport with their cameras when I came off the plane in Salt Lake City. As I sat at the terminal waiting to board my flight, I wondered if I should call the third Utah TV station and let them know I was coming. But it seemed dumb to call—I had never talked to anyone at that TV station, and I felt completely stupid calling out of the blue and saying I was Delys Cowles and were they interested in when my plane was landing. It was too weird, so I didn't call.

On the flight home, I looked around at the people sitting near me. I wondered what they would think when this normal, middle-aged woman got off the plane with TV cameras following her. As I came down the ramp, someone shouted, "There she is." The lights were on and the cameras rolled while I ran to Marissa and Steven, my two youngest children. My older three didn't want to be on camera, so they didn't come to the airport. My mother and father were waiting, and after I talked to the reporters for a while, we drove home to Provo.

I got to spend the evening talking to my children and getting an update on their lives the last few weeks. We watched ourselves on the news and got ready for bed. Immediately after the two news stations showed stories about David, a reporter from the third channel called me. It was about 10:30 P.M. He wanted to know why I hadn't called him, and could he interview me the next day. I agreed that he could interview me at my office.

The next day my parents took the airport shuttle to Salt Lake City and flew back to Los Angeles, and I got everyone off to school. Finally, I arrived at my office only about fifteen minutes before my first class. There in front of my office door was a reporter and an Eyewitness News cameraman. I agreed to do an interview on the spot. Then they asked if they could follow me and tape me teaching my first class. I agreed. Unfortunately, my daughter Cristie had my keys, and I had brought David's keys, so I ended up with a key to my office but not to my files.

"Oh, no." I quietly winced. "All my lecture notes are locked in the file drawers and I am going to give a lecture off the top of my head, with cameras recording everything." I was a little bit stressed.

But then something wonderful happened. As I walked down the hall to pick up my rolls from my mailbox, I ran across faculty member after faculty member. Everyone had followed David's progress closely, and every person had prayed for us. It took me ten minutes to walk down a short hall because I got to hug so many people. One of my good friends was telling me how much he loved my family, when he looked up and saw a TV camera filming everything he was saying in close-up. Flustered, he continued, and gave me a big hug.

When I got to my classroom door, I realized I had never met this class before. I poked my head in and said, "Does anyone mind being filmed for television news?" No one replied, but they looked rather perplexed. I opened the door wide, and walked in with a reporter and television cameraman behind me. What an entrance! I told them the story of my husband's illness and why there had been a substitute for a week, and the cameraman wandered around taking shots of students and of me. After half an hour the camera crew left, and I continued to teach about the history of the English language in a less public setting.

Back at home, life got harder. The insurance estimator suggested I call Stone Maintenance to act as a general contractor to repair all the water damage. The Stone Maintenance man looked at our cottage-cheese ceiling and told me he suspected it contained asbestos. A few days later an inspector came and confirmed his suspicions. Our ceiling was full of asbestos, and they would have to remove it in an environmentally safe way. Stone Maintenance and a piano technician moved all of our instruments and furniture from the front room to the undamaged family room. We were wall-to-wall organs, pianos, couches, and book shelves, although there was still one narrow trail leading through to the kitchen.

I didn't want to be sleeping at our home if there was going to be asbestos floating around, so Beth Hedengren's parents kindly offered us their vacant condominium a few blocks away. I moved my five children and a few clothes over to their spacious condo. Every day I drove each person to school, then went to the university to teach, then met everyone back at our house after school, then drove back to the condo. We couldn't really cook—our kitchen was buried as deeply in things from other rooms as the rest of the house—so church families signed up to feed the Cowles family. We went to a different home each night for dinner. What a treat for a mother who thinks that any meal cooked by someone else tastes wonderful! We stopped by our house on the way home and called David (there was no phone at the condo), and then we went to the condo to do homework and go to bed. David was still very weak and could hardly hold a phone up for very long. I let one child a night talk to Daddy, then I got an update on his progress. After a while he became quite lonely, and he was still nauseated.

I had my friends announce at church that the men in space suits wandering around our house were removing asbestos, *not* fumigating for flesh-eating bacteria.

After the cottage-cheese stuff was scraped from our ceiling, the contractors had to resurface the ceilings, paint the walls, and put in new carpet. We discovered that the damage extended to an upstairs bedroom, hall, and bathroom, so workers were all over the house. I spent any extra minutes shopping for carpet with my friend Julie. I tried to choose something I would like for many years and something that would match the rather dated rust carpet in the rest of our home. I chose a light sand color, and we decided we would be a shoes-off-in-the-living-room family.

On my birthday, February 9, I called David. He had no idea it was my birthday—he had no real sense of time yet—and I didn't feel like reminding him. He was feeling awful, and the most recent skin graft surgery was not as successful as the doctors had hoped. Only part of the graft "took." We talked about when he could come home. It looked as if he might be able to leave the hospital in late February or early March, but he would be too weak to fly home. I left the conversation feeling sad and wandered through my torn-up house looking at messes everywhere. I started to cry. What has happened to my life? I thought. Then I had to explain my tears to a perplexed painter.

On Valentine's Day, I walked out the back door to see a dozen long-stemmed roses. "From David," said the card. I knew someone else was behind this one because David had no way to get me flowers by himself. It turned out that Joyce Baggerly at the English Department office had called David, and the two had conspired to send me that beautiful expression of love. I smiled all day.

During January and February I flew to Los Angeles every other weekend to be with David. Neighbors took the younger children, and the older ones stayed alone at home. My visits to David really raised his spirits and helped him try harder, but my absences were hard on my children. They were under a lot of pressure from school and extracurricular activities, plus we had lived for several weeks in a condo, and now our house was torn up and piled with furniture. The children were all shaken up with the tragedy of their father's illness, and I spent hours in the evenings just talking to help everyone through. It didn't help that we were a very public family now, and everyone knew and asked about David wherever we went. We appreciated people's concern, but my children didn't like all the publicity.

Once in early February I took Marissa with me to California for a weekend trip. We visited David in the hospital on Marissa's fourth birthday. My mother had wisely bought some presents for David to give to her. Sadly, Marissa developed bronchitis in Los Angeles, and she couldn't fly home with me, so my mother offered to keep Marissa in Hacienda Heights until I returned the next week. Marissa recovered, and I flew home with her later.

Television and newspaper reporters called our house every few days to ask for interviews and updates. I wouldn't let anyone interview David while he was in Critical Care because he was too weak and too groggy. I saw no dignity in interviewing someone in a hospital bed.

One day Paul Murphy of Channel 4 called me and said he hadn't needed to bother us for information because a close friend of our family had been calling the station with regular updates.

"Who is this friend of our family?" I asked.

"I don't know, let me look up his name—it's Joe."

"I have hundreds of friends and none of them is named Joe."

"It is Joe Stone."

"I don't know anyone by that name."

I thought about it for several days. Then I noticed the Stone Maintenance trucks in front of our house, so I asked one of the workers who the owner of Stone Maintenance was.

"Joe Stone," he informed me.

I remember meeting him once when we set up the original contract for the work, but not since then. I supposed the painters must have passed information on to him and he passed it on to the television stations.

I chuckled about this one for a long time.

Highs and Lows

I sometimes got very lonely in the hospital, especially on the few occasions when Delys and my parents had to be out of town at the same time. Delys's parents came every day, which helped. Eva and Danny Thron came when they could, but they lived two hours from the hospital, and they both worked.

One day I was feeling a bit more discouraged than usual. Dr. Shin stopped by about midday.

"How are you feeling today?" he said.

"Oh, about the same."

He stopped a minute, apparently assessing the situation.

I decided just to let it out. "I guess it's getting a little frustrating. Progress seems so slow. And I still can't keep any food down. I'll probably feel better tomorrow, but I'm a little discouraged at the moment."

Dr. Shin began with the usual consolations: "Actually, you're making excellent progress. You're way ahead of where anyone thought you'd be at this point."

"Yes, I realize that. And don't think I'm not pleased. But in some ways that just makes it worse. Every time I feel I'm progressing, I want to jump to the end and be completely recovered."

"Yes, I understand. But you'll have to be patient. And remember, recovery isn't a steady climb straight up. You'll have periods of plateaus where you don't feel like you're making any progress at all. You'll have good days and bad days. You have to expect that."

"I know that in my head," I said. "But sometimes my heart doesn't care."

Dr. Shin seemed to gather his thoughts for a minute. Then for the first time he shared something very personal with me.

"I'd like to tell you about my son," he began. I came to full attention.

"Some time ago, my son was diagnosed with a rare form of stomach cancer. He underwent a long and intensive treatment of chemotherapy."

"Oh," I said. Dr. Shin's voice was quiet and obviously emotional, and it held my attention fully.

"My wife and I tried to get him to stay home from school that year to recover, but he insisted on attending school despite the pain and nausea from the chemotherapy. He worked very hard, and we sometimes wondered if he had made the wrong decision. But he kept at it, even when he was at his worst. His grades weren't as high as they had been before, but he got Bs and graduated with his class. Now he's at medical school, doing very well."

"Wow," I said. "That's really impressive."

"The point is that my son didn't just sit around. He forced himself to get out of bed and get his mind on something other than his condition."

So what's he trying to tell me, I wondered.

"What we need to do with you now, I think, is get you out of bed as much as possible."

Thinking of my recent attempts at walking, I wondered how I could possibly do that. For heaven's sake, I couldn't even get out of bed without the help of at least two strong nurses. Even then it was anybody's guess whether I'd end up standing or clumped on the floor like a pile of dirty clothes.

"How much can you do out of your bed?" Dr. Shin asked.

"Well, twice a day a therapist comes in, helps me out of bed, and takes me for a walk with my walker. I can't go very fast or very far, but I go a little farther every day. This morning I got to the far end of the desk and back, but it pretty well wiped me out for the rest of the day, I think. I'll try again this afternoon, though."

"Good," he said. "What about sitting up in a chair?"

"I haven't tried that yet. I did manage to use the portable toilet next to the bed once, but it took two nurses to get me off it, and they almost dropped me in before I could get back into the bed."

"That's a good start," he said. "Try to sit in a chair a couple of times a day and stay there as long as you can. And keep your bed as close to a sitting position as you can stand. Perhaps you could start by eating your meals sitting up."

I felt doubtful. Generally, I couldn't get my meals down at all, in any position. "I'm not sure whether I can do that, but I'll give it my best effort."

"Great," Dr. Shin said with enthusiasm. "I'll see you again tomorrow and you can tell me how you did."

After Dr. Shin left, I thought a long time about his son. His determination inspired me and made me feel embarrassed at having been discouraged. I felt renewed energy and determination.

That afternoon I walked even farther than I had in the morning. I got past the desk and about halfway to the door at the end of the Critical Care Unit. As I passed (very slowly), I noticed patients in other rooms in the unit, obviously critically ill, many with sad-eyed relatives trying to act cheerful. I was shocked at their condition, and I knew I must have looked even worse just a few short weeks before.

Stephanie was pleased with my efforts at walking and congratulated me on my progress. I don't think either of us was entirely confident in my ability to get back to the bed, however.

As I turned and started back, I heard clapping and cheering behind me. I lumbered around with the walker and saw Dr. John and his current entourage of beautiful interns (this group was from China, I think) smiling broadly and applauding loudly. I felt slightly embarrassed at this, but I appreciated the encouragement. I lifted my left hand (the good one) from the walker and waved. That probably wasn't a completely rational move, and I would undoubtedly have fallen had Stephanie not grabbed my arm. Then, knowing I had an audience, I mustered up all my strength and willpower and made it all the way back to bed. Stephanie helped me in, and I collapsed in utter exhaustion and complete happiness.

The next morning Dr. John stopped by my room. "Seeing you walking out there yesterday absolutely made my day," he said. "I could hardly believe my eyes. We just had to stop and cheer for you."

Later, when Dr. Shin came by, I had raised the bed to a near-sitting position to eat lunch. I was pleased that he came right then, because I was exhausted and about to fall over. "Thank you for sharing your son's story with me yesterday," I said. "It has inspired me to work even harder and to stay positive."

He smiled. "I'm glad it helped," he said.

. . .

On one weekend visit I brought an important letter with me.

"Guess what you just won."

"Publisher's Clearing House?"

"No, much better. Read this." The letter announced that David had been chosen by graduating English majors as their most influential teacher.

"They voted before you got sick, so this is not a sympathy vote. Considering there are seventy-five English professors at Brigham Young University, and considering that the department is full of wonderful teachers, this is a great honor."

David was extremely pleased. This was the third time in the last four years he had received this award. He started to realize how much he missed teaching that semester and how much he missed his students. I announced the award to everyone who walked in the door so they could ooh and ahh for him.

By this time David could move his fingers independently, and we were all very pleased. But he had lost so much muscle and tissue that the doctors were unsure how much he would eventually be able to use his arm.

"It's quite possible that he will be able to sign his name and that's it," Dr. Britto again told me on the side. "We just don't know what he will be able to do."

David would work his fingers and arms every day. He had lost skin and tissue about an inch deep on most of his arm, and the skin from his thighs that they used as grafts was much thinner. As David moved his arm, you could see the muscles move under his skin.

"Do you think I'll be able to play the piano?" David asked Dr. Shin one day.

"I have no idea. You can move your fingers, but we'll have to wait and see." He sounded doubtful, but he obviously didn't want to discourage David.

"What about tennis."

Oh, no, don't ask about tennis, David. Don't push it, I thought. For heaven's sake, he was missing most of the triceps in his right arm and a major muscle on his right side. He probably couldn't even hold a racquet. Obviously, tennis was gone.

"I think I can safely say that you won't be playing tennis anymore," said Dr. Shin.

"Oh, I think I can," said David.

"Well, yes, you might swing the racquet, but you will play like an old man with no power and not much of a swing."

And no serve, I thought to myself.

"Did you say I won't be able to play tennis?" David asked.

"You might be able to swing a racquet but not very well," replied Dr. Shin.

"I don't believe you. I hereby challenge you to a game of tennis. After I am recovered, I am going to visit you and play tennis against you. And I am going to win."

"I accept your challenge," Dr. Shin said, smiling. "And I sincerely hope you win."

David continued to work hard on his arm movement. On February 2, his father came to feed him breakfast, and David told him he had a birthday present for him.

"I couldn't buy you anything, so I am giving you the best present I can think of. I've been practicing all day."

David lifted his right arm, slowly brought his hand close to his face, and with considerable shaking and straining touched his thumb to his nose.

His dad cried.

. . .

One day while Delys was with me, Dr. John, the pharmacist, came in. He was obviously excited about something but seemed hesitant to talk about it.

Finally he said, "I've been thinking hard about your nausea problem. I researched everywhere I could think to look, and finally something hit me. This is just like the feelings I got about you during surgery that always turned out to be just the right thing. I think it may be the answer we've been looking for. But I'm not sure how you'll feel about it."

That puzzled me. Surely I was ready to try virtually anything, up to and including a stomach transplant.

"What did you have in mind?" Delys asked.

"Well," he said, "I know you are very religious, so you might find this totally inappropriate. But it works on a completely different principle from everything else we've tried, and I think it could do the trick."

By this time my short attention span was overloading from the suspense. "What is it?" I couldn't imagine what he could possibly mean.

Dr. John paused. Then he grinned and said, "Marijuana."

Delys and I both laughed. "You've got to be kidding," Delys said.

"No, for once I'm being serious. But it's not what you're thinking. This comes in pill form; you don't smoke it. It has no real side effects. Well, it does produce a mild euphoria in about 20 percent of those who take it. But I'm not sure that's a bad thing in this case. It's officially an experimental drug, and it's carefully controlled by the state. It's quite legal in California, though I don't know about Utah." He paused again as we took this in. "I hope I haven't

offended you in suggesting this. If you feel it's not appropriate, I'll keep searching for something else. I really don't think I'll find anything else that will work as well, though."

Delys looked at me.

"I'm ready to try almost anything if it will let me eat again," I said.

Delys agreed. "I don't see any problem with that. Though we'll have a hard time explaining it to our church leaders back home." She smiled wryly at this thought.

Dr. John seemed delighted. "Good. I found some marijuana pills stashed away in the pharmacy. They are nearly expired, which tells you how seldom anyone uses this stuff. And I have to tell you, I had to do some fast talking to get the other doctors on your team to approve this for you. But when I reminded them how long this nausea has lasted and how little effect anything else has had, they finally agreed to let you try it."

He poked two pills out of the packet. "Take these now, and I'll be back in a couple of hours to see if they have had any effect."

The effect was quick and decisive. From that time on I could eat more or less normally. And I did it with gusto. The pills had no euphoric effect on me. That made me feel slightly cheated, though just being able to eat without throwing up made me experience something approaching euphoria. The nausea returned occasionally for several months afterward, but it never again approached the levels or constancy it had before.

The next morning Delys brought Marissa to say good-bye. They were returning home, and Marissa wouldn't be back. I cried (as usual) to think how much I would miss her—how much I missed all my children. I wanted to show Delys how far I could walk now—all the way down the hall and back (about one hundred feet). As I sat in the chair preparing myself mentally for the walk, we had a surprise visit from Ted and Liz Anderson, friends from Provo. Our twelve-year-old sons were good friends. The Andersons were in town and came to visit and to bring greetings from many of our friends in Provo. They assured us that everyone in our part of the city was praying for us and our family.

In our discussion about how I was doing, I mentioned that I had just eaten my first full breakfast in some time, and that I felt stronger now that the nausea was mostly gone.

"How did you kick the nausea?" Ted asked.

Delys and I looked at each other. We both realized I had unthinkingly opened a door we didn't really want anyone to come through. For one thing, we weren't sure *we wanted to face all the kidding we would get back home if we let the news out.*

"Uh, it was a new experimental drug," I said evasively.

"Great," Ted said. "What is it called?"

We paused. Then we laughed. "Marijuana pills," Delys said.

The Andersons thought this was the funniest thing they had ever heard, and laughed so hard I thought they might soon need medical attention.

"It's okay," Delys said. "He didn't inhale. He's still eligible to be president."

About a week later I received a box in the mail from the Andersons. It was a "Marijuana Environment Kit" designed to put me in the mood for my pills. It included a pair of John Lennon glasses with purple lenses, a pile of paper flowers to spread around me, and a box of incense.

Great Escapes

One weekend in February, I flew from Salt Lake City to Los Angeles to be with David for a few days. We decided to have him stay a little longer in the hospital and have another skin graft operation that would just about cover the remaining open spots. This was discouraging because David had to be careful not to move his body much for about ten days after each skin graft operation. It felt as if he had to take one step back to make two steps forward.

As I walked back to David's room in the Critical Care Unit, I noticed that for the first time he was not hooked up to anything. Temporarily, he was not on any pain medications, antibiotics, or nutritional supplements (thanks to the amazing effects of the marijuana pills). He had no wires connected to his chest monitoring his heart, or to his fingers monitoring his oxygen. He wasn't hooked up to extra oxygen coming through his nose. Nothing.

So my scheming mind kicked in. If he is not hooked up to anything, then maybe he is mobile. I knew he could sit up for maybe thirty minutes at a time, and so perhaps my plan would work. I talked to his nurse, Vivian.

"Is there any way we could put David in a wheelchair and take him outside?"

"Hmmm. That's not normally what we do with Critical Care patients, but it sounds like a good idea."

She found a wheelchair, got permission, and we told David we were going to sneak him out of the hospital to see the outside world. His eyes lit up. He had been confined to a hospital bed since December, and now it was February. Since he was lying in a bed, he could only see a bit of the sky and had had no chance to see the beautiful courtyard three stories down.

We sat him in the chair and wrapped several layers of white blankets all around him to keep him warm and to hold him up. Vivian pushed him over to the window near the elevator and left us for a few minutes. David went crazy with delight looking at springtime out the window. There were green trees and flowers and birds and parts of the human world his eyes had longed for but had almost forgotten.

"I feel like I just got out of prison," he said.

We sat in silence for a few moments.

Outside in the quads we wandered with the wheelchair around the planters full of greenery and flowers. Because of the heavy California rains, everything was exceptionally green, and spring had come in February. The normally brownish hills in Hacienda Heights were nearly as green as the English countryside David loved. I relished the unusually luscious scenery every day as I drove over the hills to the hospital, practically singing prayers of thanks for the newness of plant life and the newness of my husband's life.

David soaked in the fresh air and the sounds of wind and birds. But after about fifteen minutes he tired, and we went inside. Before we went back to the Critical Care room, I showed him the Critical Care waiting room where our families had spent so much time. I showed him the halls I had wandered so many times. Then I took him to a different window.

"These are the elbow trees. Kathryn named them."

"I think they look like elephant legs."

"Yeah, maybe a skinny elephant. Now if you look down to that large limb closest to us and follow it to the next small branch, look carefully. Do you see that round nest about the size of a half-dollar?"

"Barely."

"That is the hummingbird's nest your mother discovered back in January. We've been watching the two birds taking turns sitting on two tiny eggs for weeks. Look, now there are two tiny baby birds in that nest."

"I can barely see them. But I'm tired now. I need to lie down."

We went back to his "cell" and helped him out of the wheelchair and onto the bed again. I left and let him sleep, knowing he had been energized by the prospects of returning to the world beyond the hospital someday.

• • •

Near the end of February, Dr. Britto gave me the usual examination.

117

"How are you feeling today?" he asked.

"Quite well," I said. "I feel like I am getting a little stronger each day."

"Well," he said, "I think you're ready for a promotion. How would you feel about moving out of the Critical Care Unit and into a regular room?"

"Sure," I said.

"You really don't need as much attention as you get up here any longer. Besides, I'm not sure we could justify keeping you here to your insurance company."

"Okay."

"We'll have them move you this afternoon, then. I'll make sure you get a room in the best section."

Wow! After six weeks in Critical Care, I had graduated. I had worked my way up from critically ill to regular sick-enough-to-be-in-the-hospital status.

Delys and Vivian, one of my favorite nurses, collected all my things—books, letters, tapes, CDs, and a huge mound of hospital stuff.

"You might as well take all this stuff," Vivian said. "You've paid for everything here, and they'll just throw it all out if you leave it."

It took multiple boxes and a cart to get everything moved. Delys had some difficulty fitting everything into the drawer space in the new room, so she took several boxes of letters and other things home.

Late that afternoon an orderly came to move me. He took my bed, all the IV stuff, and the things I still had with me. I insisted on keeping the bed. From the beginning, the doctors put me in a bed that was filled with air and constantly moving. Every two minutes one side would deflate a bit and the other side would inflate. I slept to the rhythm of right, middle, left, middle for two months. This ocean effect kept my body from ever having bed sores. I had gotten used to the constant rising and falling motion, and I felt sure it helped keep my back from aching even more than it did.

The new room was smaller than the old one, but my heart soared as I found myself next to a window looking out onto grass, trees, and a hospital parking lot. From the old room in Critical Care I could see out a window some distance away, but the view consisted of the corner of a building and a tiny patch of sky. I spent much of my time in the new room looking out the window. I especially enjoyed a distant orange tree laden with fruit. It made me feel somehow more connected to things that were healthy and alive.

It didn't take me long to notice the difference in care. Instead of one nurse for every two patients as in the Critical Care Unit, here one nurse had to cover ten

118

patients. Most of the time I didn't mind the extra privacy. But I was still unable to do much of anything without help—including getting out of bed for any reason.

I realized just how helpless I was that first night in the new room. For some reason my nurse call button mysteriously stopped working about 7:00 P.M. At first I didn't mind the fact that no one had come to check on me. I felt stupidly and euphorically independent. But after 9:30 or so, I began to feel differently. I needed help before I could go to sleep, and there was no way for me to get it. I couldn't get my toothbrush or washcloth. I couldn't arrange my things for the night. But most frustrating, I couldn't turn off the bright florescent lights. And I couldn't even doze with them on. I lay there with the television playing one inane program after another, becoming more and more exhausted with every passing minute but utterly unable to do anything to solve the problem. Finally a nurse popped her head in my door. I yelled so loudly to get her attention, I think she almost had a heart attack. She explained that since I hadn't called, they assumed everything was fine. She hadn't wanted to disturb me.

I could tell I wasn't in Kansas anymore.

As the days passed until my next surgery, and especially during the difficult period of recovery afterward when I had to be careful not to move excessively or disturb my new skin grafts, I found myself battling depression. My back ached constantly, the restrictions on my movements kept me from working to regain my stength and flexibility, and I missed my family terribly. I also came to realize how much of my identity centered on my work as a teacher. I felt as if yet another part of my deepest self lay sick along with my body, my music, my tennis, my mind.

Several things combined to help me fight this tendency to depression, however. For one thing, Delys had arranged for one friend from home to call me each afternoon. Colleagues and neighbors signed up for turns. Those conversations inevitably wore me out, but they also gave me much-needed contact with the world outside and with my real life beyond the hospital.

I also received pleasure from many visitors: Delys, her parents, Eva and Danny Thron, and occasional friends from home. I rejoiced at the continued visits of favorite nurses from the Critical Care Unit who dropped by to see me. Delys and her parents would take me for wheelchair trips whenever I was allowed to move enough to get out of bed. Those trips outside made me so happy I could hardly hold my joy inside. I even got to almost enjoy the frequent appearances of people I didn't know who came by to see "the Miracle Man."

My twice-daily bandage changes were now a comparative pleasure, since most of my gaping holes had been at least partially covered. I still had patches of skinless tissue showing all around my body where the grafts had not taken, but the days of excruciating pain were largely over—at least for a while.

Each morning and afternoon, Stephanie, Rebecca, Gina, or one of the other physical therapists would take me walking, stretch my right arm and shoulder, and generally cheer me up. I especially enjoyed walking. I worked hard to go farther each day than the day before. One day I went so far that Stephanie took my walker away from me. Though walking on my own power tired me, I was excited to discover I could get around at least a little on my own.

Several other personal triumphs also thrilled me. When you can't do much, you have to find your victories in small things. I rejoiced the day my catheter was removed and I could walk around a bit and use the bathroom alone (a frightening experience in some ways—what if I got stuck on the toilet and couldn't get up?). Or imagine my joy on the day Dr. Britto authorized me to take my first shower in over six weeks—though I had so many restrictions on what I could wash that I'm not sure I emerged much cleaner than when I entered.

Two of my therapists performed extraordinary acts of kindness that made my life better. Gina, who had been a hairdresser in her pre-physical therapy life, cut my hair twice. Joyce, who knew I needed more calories than I could eat and understood how tiring hospital food can get, got permission to bring me a blackberry milkshake from a local restaurant. It amazed me how meaningful these small acts of thoughtfulness were to me. I resolved to do more things like that for others when I got back to my normal life.

I also found I could repay some of Dr. Britto's kindness to me by making suggestions about a murder mystery he was writing in all the spare time he didn't have. The novel's protagonist was, as one might expect, a plastic surgeon. I enjoyed getting back to writing again, even if it was for someone else's book. It also turned out that Dr. Britto and I shared similar tastes in music, so we exchanged CDs and tapes.

When I had been in the regular room for three or four days, my father had a serious argument with a nurse.

This nurse, an older, obviously experienced woman, whom I will call Nurse Jones, seemed to frown whenever someone helped me cut up my food. About the fourth day in the new room, my father went out to the nurses' station to ask a question. Nurse Jones was there. She apparently felt this was the perfect opportunity to teach my father how to deal with me.

"You know," she said, looking up from some papers over the top of her glasses, "you really do too much for your son. Like when you cut up his food for him. He really needs to do as much for himself as possible. You're making it too easy for him. He seems to be something of a wimp."

That was too much for my ever-patient father.

"Do you even know why he's in here?" my father demanded.

"Well, no. Something about a skin disease, wasn't it?"

"Something like that, yes. He's had flesh-eating bacteria. He's lucky to be alive."

"That was him?" Nurse Jones said, obviously surprised. She apparently hadn't looked at my chart, which was now several inches thick.

"Did you know that he can't use his right hand at all?" my father said.

"No, I didn't. Is he right-handed?"

"Yes, he is," my father said.

"Oh," said Nurse Jones, beginning to show signs of embarrassment. "I didn't know."

"And did you know that he hates being in the hospital. He's so anxious to get out that he pushes himself harder than he should to get out a little sooner. Several times he has actually set himself back by trying to do too much too soon."

"I had no idea," Nurse Jones said. "I guess he could probably use a little help here and there."

"We come in to help him eat because nobody here will help him. He'd probably starve to death if we didn't. Believe me, if he thinks he has any chance of doing something without help, he does it."

After that, Nurse Jones was much nicer and more helpful. The day I finally left the hospital, she came in to say good-bye, though she wasn't assigned to my room that day.

"I just wanted to tell you that I think you're a very courageous man," she said. I wasn't sure how to respond, considering her earlier opinion of me.

"Thank you," I finally said. "I do my best."

Freedom!

The second day David was sick, I asked the doctors for a projection. If he lived, how long would David be in the hospital, and then what care would he need. Dr. Tuddenham said if David lived, he would probably be in the hospital for six months or so because he had lost so much skin. It would take that long to rebuild his body and cover it with skin grafts, and at least two years before full recovery—whatever that might turn out to mean.

Now it was the end of February and David had shortened his six-month sentence down to two. Not only did his body heal remarkably quickly, but 50 to 80 percent of his skin grafts "took" every time he had an operation. The doctors were able to stretch and staple much of the existing skin on his sides and his chest to cover the large four-inch gaps that were skinless. This left fewer spaces that needed skin grafts, hence a shorter stay in the hospital. There was a large skinless hole about an inch deep and an inch in diameter in his chest where the stretched skin wouldn't fully reach. His right side had large spots where the grafts never took—one was about four inches in diameter, and his right elbow area was also raw.

David was needing less and less help in the hospital, so when the last skin graft operation seemed to take well, the doctors were ready to send him home. But he couldn't come home to Utah because he couldn't climb stairs and he couldn't sit up on an airplane long enough for the ninety-minute flight. So my parents kindly agreed to let David stay at their home in Hacienda Heights until he was stronger.

We decided he could leave on February 23, a Saturday. I needed to know a week ahead of time because I knew the news people would want to be there to document his leaving. So many people had requested interviews with David, and this seemed an appropriate time. I talked to David and the public relations people at the hospital, and we decided that David would give one-on-one interviews with each station or newspaper that wanted one. In between each interview he would get a chance to lie down and rest for a few minutes. I found that one-on-one interviews are much more relaxed and calm than a press-conference setting where everyone is vying for attention. That week I called all of the TV stations who had called me, and I told them about David's discharge. David had never given an interview, although everyone wanted to interview him in the hospital. I had discouraged earlier interviews because they would wear David out. Now he was stronger and could handle the stress better.

During the week before David's release, one TV station wanted to come to film our house as we were getting ready for David's return. Stone Maintenance was still diligently working on restoring our house after the flood, and so several workers were painting the walls. I mentioned to them that Channel 5 was going to come in a few hours to film our house, and did they mind being on television. They said, "No problem." At lunch they went home and got on their official Stone Maintenance shirts. Then, as I was walking across the street to the Hedengrens' house, five large Stone Maintenance trucks drove up and parked next to the truck that had been there all month. Suddenly there were four or five new workers inside, all sporting official shirts. The camera team came and took pictures of our piano, our living room, and the workers painting the stair rails. But they never included pictures of the trucks, much to Stone Maintenance's disappointment.

I flew out Friday, and Saturday we started packing all the letters and supplies we were going to take home. These filled the entire backseat of my parents' car. Then we got David dressed in a yellow shirt and gray sweatpants—the first clothes he had worn in two months (not counting the sheets he wore for the first month and the gaping hospital gown he wore for the second). Both sets of parents were there, and when everyone was ready, David's father pushed him down the hall in the wheelchair while we followed. Cameras recorded our winding trail to the interview room. We even staged a pretended exit out the front door so it could all be on camera before the interviews.

Then our parents went into one room, Dr. Shin into another, and David and I into a third. This way we could keep three reporters busy at once. David had his sleeves rolled up and his forearms exposed. All of the cameras focused on his arm because his scars were so evident. Not only were there strips of skin grafts all over his arm, but where he had lost flesh, there were crevices up to an inch deep. That night our children in Provo watched the news and saw their father for the first time in six weeks. They also saw his scarred arm for the first time, and Cristie says the sight of Dad's severely injured arm shocked them all.

The reporters mostly talked to David, who now looked about a hundred years old, and asked him what it felt like to have this disease. Then they wanted to know how he made it through. Several reporters made the comparison with Job: "After everything you have gone through, are you beginning to feel like Job?"

"A lot of things are similar, I suppose. But in the end, Job's situation was much more difficult. His friends turned against him, but my friends have sustained me in every way possible. I've been very blessed."

David thanked people for praying for him and supporting him. Between each interview he lay down on a couch in the room. After three TV interviews, David and I and our parents returned to David's room. There he rested before granting another interview with a newspaper reporter.

My mother was worried about taking David home to her house, the very place he had contracted the illness in the first place. She asked Dr. Saketkhoo if she should do anything to prevent him from getting this disease again.

"Just forget about it. Treat him like a normal person. This bacteria is everywhere—in people's hair and in their clothes. You can't escape it. But the chances of the bacteria becoming aggressive inside his body again are very small. It is kind of like getting hit by lightning. It's a fluke."

When everything quieted down a bit, David needed to rest more, so I wandered back up to the third floor where everything began. I found a suggestion box and wrote a big thank you and compliments for the hospital volunteers who had helped us so much and who get no pay and little recognition. Then I looked out the windows for the last time. There in the crook of the elbow trees was the small hummingbird nest. The nest was bare. The babies had learned to fly and had left the nest along with the parents.

After a short rest, David climbed into the wheelchair, and we left the hospital for good.

. . .

Free at last,
Free at last,
Thank God Almighty
I'm free at last.

Waiting It Out
at the Waites'

O nce I got settled in at the Waites' house, I set about the
serious business of recovering enough to fly home to
Provo. I was determined to get back before my birthday
on March 19. That was less than three weeks away, and I
knew I was not nearly ready for the long flight and the
one-hour drives to and from the airports, let alone for dealing with the news
media and the many well-wishers I knew would be waiting for me.

*Much of the burden of taking care of me fell to my mother-in-law, June Waite.
With inexhaustible patience she changed my bandages once or twice daily—a
process involving various layers, ointments, and adhesives and taking at least half
an hour each time. Because much of my body was still oozing despite the skin
grafts, June also had to daily wash my sheets, pajamas, and any clothing I wore.
She or Merwin drove me back to the hospital for therapy sessions three times each
week. June walked behind me with the wheelchair whenever I went walking outside
(once or twice daily in good weather).*

*Special physical arrangements were required as well. I took over Merwin's
favorite family-room recliner in front of the television, as well as the nearby
couch when I couldn't sit up any longer. June put a plastic chair in the shower so
I could sit while bathing.*

*The three weeks I spent with my in-laws involved daily workouts and small
triumphs, enormous efforts, and tiny improvements each day, followed by general
exhaustion for many hours.*

. . .

At the hospital, the physical therapists taught me how to change David's
bandages. At home at night, I taught my mother. Eventually the routine
became Neosporin, Adaptic (greased gauze), pads, dry gauze, then stretchy

126

conforming bandages taped on to hold it all in place. There were spots all over his chest, sides, and especially his arm where the skin grafts had not taken. These all needed to be bandaged several times a day. We even learned how to use sterile gloves. As the next few weeks went on, my mother noticed that the largest open spot on David's side looked a lot like a map of the United States. As skin grafts heal, they can spread a little bit and close up surrounding wounds. A week later my mother called and said the wound had lost Baja California, and a week after that Texas and Florida were fading quickly.

.   .   .

Three events from this time stand out as moving and particularly significant to me.

After recovering from the ride home from the hospital on the Saturday I made my escape, I didn't try to play the piano right away. I think I feared the emotional disappointment if my hands refused to cooperate.

My right arm still moved only through a very limited range of motion, and my right hand, so long immobilized, had very little strength and less coordination. It had improved to the extent that it was basically a toss-up whether to sign hospital forms with my right hand or my left. Both bore as little resemblance as possible to my previous signature. I held little hope that I could play the piano. Though I never told anyone, deep down inside I feared I might never regain my ability to play.

Before I went near my in-laws' piano, I carefully assessed the situation and tried to control how I would respond in the event of a musical disaster. I decided that if I could just play two notes together, I would consider it a victory and try to be enthusiastic about that. But I knew almost any result would leave me disappointed and frustrated.

Late that afternoon, when Delys's parents had left to do some shopping, I announced to Delys that I was ready to try the piano. We both sensed the importance of this moment. I adjusted the bench, and Delys sat on a chair next to the piano.

I put my hands to the keys, but I hesitated. This moment really frightened me.

First I tried a simple five-note scale with my right hand. I was surprised to discover that I didn't do nearly as badly as I had expected.

Then I tried a couple of two-note thirds. That went relatively well, too.

I stopped and looked over at Delys. I don't think either of us breathed.

127

Then my hands dropped into well-remembered patterns. I seemed to watch from a distance, as if they belonged to someone else, as they began creating real music. I improvised on a slow pattern of jazzy major seventh chords. My hands moved up and down the keys with a facility that certainly didn't equal my previous abilities but which far exceeded anything I could even have hoped for from them.

I stopped playing and looked at Delys. We both cried for some time.

The physical and emotional efforts left me exhausted, so I had to go lie down then. But I will always remember the moment I first made music again as one of the most moving and significant of my life.

What little energy I had left over the next few days I seemed to spend performing for everyone who came by: Delys's parents, Eva and Danny Thron, several sets of neighbors. Many of them also cried, sharing my joy.

Sunday, February 24, was my mother's birthday. Now that I had escaped from the hospital, my parents finally felt it was time to return to Portland and begin putting their interrupted lives back together. They booked a flight home early Monday morning. Sunday night they stopped by the Waite home to drop off some pajamas they had purchased for me and to say good-bye.

As with my father's birthday several weeks earlier, I had no purchased gift to offer my mother. So I invited her into the front room and told her I had a surprise. She sat in the same chair by the piano that Delys had used the day before. When I began playing, she wept with joy, which continued for many minutes. Even my normally stoic father shed tears. My mother said it was the best birthday present she had ever received, and I'm certain it was the best one I ever gave.

Monday morning Merwin insisted I record some of my early piano playing. That afternoon when I went back to the hospital for my first physical therapy visit as an outpatient, I brought the tape and my personal cassette player and headphones.

Rebecca worked with me that day. Before we began the torture part of my visit, I told her I had a surprise. She put the headphones over her ears, and I pushed the play button. Though I couldn't hear the music myself, I could certainly see the effect it had on her. Her eyes filled. Finally she removed the headphones. She tried to talk but couldn't, so we embraced to express what words could never communicate.

"Let me take this to Stephanie," Rebecca said. She returned a few minutes later, smiling mischievously.

"I didn't tell her what it was. I just said you wanted her to hear."

A minute or two later Stephanie hurried in, headphones on her ears, wiping tears from her face. I remember thinking how I wished all my music had such powerful effects on listeners. We hugged, too, and the three of us exulted in what we all felt was yet another miracle.

Within a few days I began sight-reading classical pieces and doing finger exercises. Before the first week was over, one-finger exercise had worked itself into my first new composition (though hopefully no one will ever notice its prosaic origin). For some time I didn't play through any of my old compositions but only worked on new ones. I felt I had begun a new life that demanded new musical expressions.

The second especially memorable event from my time at the Waites' nearly scared my in-laws to death. Despite the marijuana pills, I still had trouble with nausea while eating, especially late in the day. June tried to cook fairly bland meals so they wouldn't make me sick, but my system often refused to accept any nourishment.

The doctors had now decided that the whole pharmacy of antibiotics they had given me had killed all the digestive bacteria in my stomach, and that this was probably causing my eating difficulties. Eventually the problem would solve itself as the bacteria slowly returned. In the meantime, nausea was just one more thing I would have to put up with. Still, I managed to keep down enough food to gain back a few pounds of my lost flesh. (By the way, getting flesh-eating bacteria is a very effective way to take off a few pounds, but I'm afraid I can't recommend it as a weight-loss program for general use.)

One day, about a week before I was supposed to fly home, my nausea suddenly became extreme, accompanied by severe body aches. In fact, my symptoms seemed unsettlingly familiar. My shocked in-laws were afraid the flesh-eating disease had struck again.

As the symptoms continued, the Waites became even more concerned. It took them longer to contact Dr. Saketkhoo than they wished. In the meantime, though I was extremely sick, I wasn't particularly worried. On the one hand, I knew that if I had somehow contracted necrotizing fasciitis again, there was really no point in worrying. I was a dead man, pure and simple. There was no way my body could handle that disease again in its weakened condition. What's more, if I had the disease again, I would much rather have died then and there than have faced the whole ordeal another time.

On the other hand, I couldn't believe everything that had happened—the many miracles of my survival and recovery—could possibly end with the disease finally winning at this late date. I maintained a quiet confidence that all this had been for a purpose, though I didn't know for certain what that was. I knew God wouldn't change his mind now.

Eventually my in-laws made contact with Dr. Saketkhoo. He understood their concerns, but he assured them that people didn't get this disease twice. "David is no more at risk than anyone else," he told them. "The odds of getting this thing again are so small as to be impossible. Don't worry. He'll get better. Just be patient."

That comforted my in-laws somewhat, but I don't think either of them breathed easy until I finally showed signs of recovery several days later. I still don't know what caused the frightening symptoms, but they passed a couple of days before I was to depart for Provo, leaving me somewhat weakened but even more confident of my eventual recovery.

The third memorable event from my time with the Waites occurred the last day I returned to the hospital for a therapy session. I brought boxes of candy and other gifts for some of the therapists and nurses who had helped me in so many ways. But, as usual, they outdid me. They had ordered a cake, brought in ice cream and drinks, and threw a party with many of those who knew me best. Even in my excitement about going home, I knew I would miss these friends from my darkest time.

During the next days, my practical in-laws kept pointing out that I could easily delay my flight home. Even I could see some wisdom in doing that, though I wouldn't admit it then. I would not even entertain the idea of postponing my return. I kept working hard on my strength and endurance. Finally, the day before I was to leave, I accomplished the considerable triumph of walking around the entire block unassisted. I fairly shone with pride and joy.

On March 17, two days before my forty-first birthday, the Waites drove me to the airport. Since there were no places to lie down in the airport, I rested in the car until the last possible moment to conserve energy. The Waites wheeled me to the boarding gate and waved as a flight attendant wheelchaired me onto the plane. Though I was already tired and faced the prospect of an exhausting journey, my spirits soared higher than the plane. The last stage of my recovery was beginning, and I could see ahead the promise of a joyful and worthwhile life. And I desired that more than anything I had ever wanted before.

Homecoming

While David was at my parents' home building up the strength to fly home, I was in Provo teaching full-time at the university, remodeling our home because of the flood, teaching four piano students, and raising Cristie, Kathryn, Rob, Steven, and Marissa. Each of our children needed attention, and they continued many of their extracurricular activities.

Cristie, a high school senior, wouldn't go back to school after Christmas until she knew her father was going to be all right. Then she found comfort in talking about the ordeal to whoever asked. She had many student government and chamber choir activities. At the same time she had senioritis and didn't really want to go to school that last semester, although she maintained wonderful grades. Cristie also appreciated having Dad's car to drive to school while he was in California.

Kathryn, a sophomore, was cast in Shakespeare's *A Midsummer Night's Dream* at the high school. This meant many extra trips to pick her up after practices. Kathryn was really shaken up by David's sickness and suffered a lot silently. She basically withdrew for about three weeks and wouldn't talk to anyone about her father's illness. She did not like people asking her about her father, and she did not want anyone to feel sorry for her. She composed exquisite guitar songs about her traumas.

Rob, in middle school, was busy with intensive piano lessons and soccer practices. He practiced on an electric piano at the condo and whatever keyboard he could climb to as our house was being redone. He tried to find places to practice his saxophone where he wouldn't disturb people with the noise. Rob hated the publicity the most, and he ran to the neighbor's

131

house to hide whenever reporters were around.

Steven, in third grade, didn't mind the publicity. When he went to school, his friends said, "I saw you on TV last night. You're famous." He kind of liked the extra attention. His third-grade class made a paper chain to help him anticipate his father's homecoming. Because my mind was distracted in many different directions, I didn't have much time to help him with piano or reading. He got a football for Christmas and was sad his father wasn't able to play with him anymore.

Marissa, in preschool, got to see her father a lot because I took her on friends-fly-free flights. Then I had to leave her in California when she became quite ill, so she got to be with both sets of grandparents and her daddy. Even with all of the shuffling around, she remained secure, especially if she had her kiki, or blanket, and if mommy held her a lot and listened to her lengthy conversations.

And who did I talk to? I went walking twice a week with my friend Beth. Because the ground was covered with snow, we packed up the stroller and took off to the mall twice a week early in the morning. We exercised by walking and talking.

Several months later Marissa needed some socks, so I drove her to the store to buy some.

"We are going to stop at the mall and buy you some socks."

A long pause.

"You can buy things at the mall?" she asked.

"Yes, it is full of stores."

"Oh, I thought it was just for walking."

During these unusually stressful months, I felt capable and peaceful. We prayed as a family just about every night, and we read scriptures when we were together. We also felt buoyed up by the faith and prayers of other people who prayed not only for David but also for his family.

As the time grew close for David to come home, I hurried to get the house ready for him. My good friends came and helped hang blinds; other friends made and hung curtains in the refinished rooms. Stone Maintenance had beautifully finished the front room, hall, and bedroom. All the furniture was back in place, and we were beginning to feel normal again.

The whole neighborhood came to celebrate David's homecoming. Friends arrived early in the day and hung "Welcome Back, David" signs and covered the yard with yellow balloons and yellow ribbons. At the front entrance to the yard they hung a large yellow balloon arch. Inside I was trying to finish the last-minute cleaning, but I had to cut it short to go to the airport. I drove our family to the airport in record speed because we were running late, and it would be just too embarrassing to have all of these TV cameras and David but no family to welcome him. We ran all the way to the gate.

When we arrived, people were deplaning, so we stood in anticipation of the last person arriving in a wheelchair. All the cameras were on us. But David never came. Finally, one of the cameramen pointed out that we were at the wrong gate. We moved over to the correct gate nonchalantly, trying not to look like we just made a big, stupid mistake. Another family from our church arrived to welcome David with us, and some of the newspeople interviewed Cristie.

Then David's plane finally arrived. Once again, we grouped together as a family looking for the wheelchair with David. People getting off the plane stared at the mass of cameras wondering what or who was happening with this flight. Then we saw a flight attendant pushing a wheelchair, and as it arrived with David safely in it, we all had a group hug. Except for Marissa, the children had not seen David since that first week in the hospital. Everyone got a hug and a kiss, and I took a very long hug and kiss. Here was my husband, finally back home. We cheered to have David back. Earlier we had asked the reporters to save questions for later in the day at our home so we wouldn't tire David. Consequently, the cameras rolled but without the usual interviews.

We pushed David back to the car, which was conveniently parked in the handicapped space, thanks to our new handicapped sticker. The other family from our church called ahead to Provo to warn the welcomers that we were on our way. I drove slowly so we would be the last ones there. As we neared our street, I warned David that there was going to be a big celebration at our house.

"How big?" he asked.

"Big," I answered.

As we drove down a side street, David caught a glimpse of the yellow-clad house complete with about a 150 people in the yard.

"I don't think I'm ready for all this attention."

"Get used to attention, sweetheart."

I drove around the block to buy him time. Then I drove down the most visible street right to our driveway. Everyone cheered when David stepped out of the car and into the waiting wheelchair. He was overwhelmed by the support. Little by little, people of all ages stepped up to shake David's hand and give him a hug. One family made a poster for him. Small children gave him cards. When everyone had greeted him, I pushed him to the front of the house. We went under the balloon arch and up to the front door. Then with cameras filming and everyone watching, David stood up and approached the front stairs.

"I'd better make it, hadn't I?" he quipped.

He walked up the front stairs by himself. Another cheer. I kissed him on the front porch, and we waved to everyone like a king and queen on a balcony.

Then he walked into the living room and seemed to hear our wonderful grand piano calling his name. With the doors open so everyone could hear, and with all the TV cameras on him, David played a piece he had composed in California. Everyone was amazed that his fingers and hands and arms worked well enough to play the piano.

In the interviews afterwards, one reporter asked three-year-old Marissa what it was like when her daddy was gone.

"We weren't a family," she answered.

Now that your daddy is back, what does it feel like?

"We're a family."

That night I looked over at David lying next to me in bed. It felt odd yet very comfortable to be this close to him again. I had gone almost three months without a husband around, and now I could only smile and pray thankful prayers.

Over the next few weeks people continued to help our family. One neighbor who had written David nearly every day came over to sit with him while I went to work that first week. Another dropped by to take David for his daily short walk. People donated to our trust fund, and several gave us money to help pay for the many plane flights, supplies, and medical costs. Colleagues sent him books on tape and videos. Some sent flowers.

David gradually got used to his celebrity status, but not at first. We went to a department store to buy him some shirts that he could easily wear over his bandages. As I pushed him in a wheelchair, a lady we didn't know recognized David from television. She approached him and felt like she had to say something:

"I've just got to tell you, you'll do anything to get a little publicity."

We all laughed. It seemed everywhere we went, people knew who we were and stopped us to ask questions or to offer encouragement. We appreciated the good wishes, though it took twice as long to do anything than it would have otherwise.

David's return to the BYU English Department one sunny day in April was also joyous. In past years he had always tried to gather people together to eat lunch. This time he dropped in on the department unannounced, wheelchaired to his colleagues' office doors, and announced, "Lunch." He went up and down the hall hugging his fellow teachers who had prayed so much for him.

Pain and
Physical Terrorism

The next months were a process of pain, determination, gradual recovery, exploration of my new body and what it could (and couldn't) do, and great kindness from many people. If any one thing typified my recovery process, I suppose it would have to be pain.

For starters, it seemed as if everything hurt: ribs, back, arm, and especially my right elbow. I got (and still get occasionally) phantom pains in places where I usually had no feeling, and horrible itches in places I could not feel to scratch. I spent as much time as I could lifting embarrassingly light weights and walking, typically followed by sore muscles and general exhaustion for the rest of the day. But I was determined to recover as quickly as possible and to regain the life I had lost.

Most of the pain I experienced was beyond my control. For one thing, I required three more operations before all the skin grafts (except the stubborn right elbow) finally "took" and my insides were completely encompassed by skin again. I recognized that in my case, recovering meant re-covering me with skin. But I hated these last surgeries. The operations themselves didn't bother me; I had grown so accustomed to the process by now that I hardly felt any apprehension at all. They had become routine. Before the last two I didn't even remember to call loved ones to inform them of times and dates.

What I hated were the side effects. Each encounter with anaesthesia seemed to re-numb my recovering brain. I knew that after surgery I wouldn't be able to think straight for several weeks. And who knew how long the less obvious effects would last? The phrase "We're just going to put you to sleep now" was a blatant euphemism. If I had merely been asleep, the pain of slicing skin off my legs and stapling it onto my arm and torso would certainly have awakened me. Anaesthesia doesn't make the brain go to sleep; it turns it off. The effects of that always frustrated me. My mind had always been my strongest asset, and I hated to have its capacities severely reduced every time it seemed to be coming back into its own.

The operations also caused physical frustrations. For one thing, Dr. Hirsche, my plastic surgeon in Provo, had to immobilize my right arm for several weeks after each surgery so the grafts on my elbow—the most sensitive and hard-to-cover place—could have a fighting chance. That made me left-handed again—something I never could master with any facility. The grafts on my torso and hips had to be protected from too much movement as well. So my efforts at physical recovery slid backward while my skin recovered. The emotional side of recovery isn't so hard when you can see yourself making progress. But each new operation seemed to involve several large steps back.

By far the most intense pain during my recovery occurred for several hours three times each week as I braved the prolonged attacks of Ron Nuttall, therapist extraordinaire. I discovered Ron through Jeff Fillmore, my long-time tennis partner who had done volunteer work for Ron. He told me Ron was willing to spend more time actually working on patients than any other physical therapist he knew. This literal "hands-on" time seemed exactly what I needed, so I made my first appointment as soon as I thought I could handle the trip into Ron's office.

Ron turned out to be another godsend. Generous, kind, and affable, Ron combined a deep understanding of how the body works with a profound comprehension of his patients' emotional and spiritual needs. His hands, exceptionally strong from daily workouts on patients, had the ability to feel what they should do. Ron also had another gift: he wasn't afraid to hurt me to help me heal faster. He discovered that much of my inability to bend and stretch occurred because of scarring deep beneath my skin grafts. On my right side, particularly, where I had lost all the padding between grafted skin and the remaining muscles and bones beneath, the scars had adhered to my ribs and muscles and would not stretch. Normally skin moves freely over ribs and hips. Mine was stuck firmly to them.

During each session Ron would patiently work these scars. He pressed hard with his thumbs, then worked them past each other to break up the scar tissue as deeply as possible. This was as painful as anything I have ever experienced, with the possible exception of daily debridements in the hospital. Then Ron stretched me. He would pull my body in every conceivable direction to encourage it to move just a little farther than the time before. Often this involved the help of an assistant, and together they would bend and pull me until I thought I would pass out from the pain. By the time I left, I was so exhausted from trying to endure the agony that I could do little else the rest of the day. I quickly learned to schedule appointments with Ron late in the day.

Trying to deal with the pain of these therapy appointments took all my concentration and self-control, which became increasingly difficult as the sessions went on and my exhaustion increased. Ron told me that different patients handle pain very differently. Some simply scream in agony at the slightest touch. One patient he remembered hadn't moved or made a sound. Ron knew how painful the process had been by the single tear that slid down from one eye. At first I attempted to hide my pain during our sessions. I tried to be stoic, probably from that latent machismo cultured into me from cowboy movies and Leave It to Beaver. I think I was pretty good at this, though the prolonged guttural grunt familiar to my therapists in the hospital had not abandoned me. I nicknamed Ron my physical terrorist.

I soon learned that during especially painful moments Ron was actually watching me slyly out of the corner of his eye to evaluate how much pain I was feeling. He wanted to push me to my limits but not beyond them. So I found ways of letting him know without actually screaming.

Ron was pleased (and surprised) to discover that his treatments did not result in excessive soreness on the days between sessions. I was surprised, too, considering what he was doing to my body. We both saw this as yet another blessing, and we made the most of it by pushing hard during our sessions.

Many medical people have commented on my positive attitude toward pain. I recognized early on that my path to recovery lay in that direction, and that the more pain I could bear, the faster I would recover. I remember thinking in the hospital that if I could knock another ten minutes off my total recovery time by experiencing a bit of pain now, it was well worth it.

It was only recently, however, that I finally understood why all the pain I have experienced did not take the emotional toll on me I might have expected. Sometimes we don't understand what we have learned—we can't put it into words, or literally come to terms with it—until later. I think this is one of the most important lessons I learned from my experience with pain.

I believe that how pain affects us depends largely on how we feel about it. I have come to realize that, at least most of the time, I chose my pain, and that

that made all the difference. If we try to hide from our pain—emotional, physical, spiritual—it will defeat us. If we try to fight it, it will eventually wear us down. But if we recognize its benefits and freely choose the pain, it becomes our friend. We accept it as a kind of gift. And, at our better moments, we can actually offer it freely as a gift to God and to those we love. Choosing to accept the pain doesn't make it hurt less, but it does change its meaning. The pain then serves us rather than the reverse.

People who have survived long periods of intense pain seem to share a bond of suffering. A colleague of mine, John S. Harris, crashed his tiny homemade airplane several years ago. He barely survived, and his agonizing recovery was long and difficult. Once athletic and daring, John now walks painfully with a cane, and his body aches constantly. John is some twenty-five years my senior, and though we often spoke in the hallways, we were never particularly close. But now we share something that most other people cannot quite comprehend.

Speaking to me a few weeks ago, John commented on this. "You never know until you have been through something like this how you will react," he said. "Facing death and experiencing horrible pain teach you things about yourself you can't know otherwise." For one thing, he said, he learned that death was only death after all. He won't be frightened of it again. For another, his struggles with pain forced him to find out just how strong he really could become. "You and I know now what we can do in ways people who haven't been through that can't," he told me. "And knowing that, we don't have to fear what may happen to us in the future." I agree.

John also helped me understand another aspect of my experience. John's accident resulted in a lot of publicity. He received more notoriety when he had nine graduate students meet him weekly in the hospital for an advanced technical writing class he insisted on teaching on schedule. When I first visited the English Department in a wheelchair, John asked me how I was adapting to the roles all the publicity was forcing on me. I don't think I quite understood then. When we discussed this more recently, he asked me the question again.

"I don't always feel comfortable with the way people sometimes treat me as if I were some sort of saint," I responded. "And I'm often puzzled by the way some people treat me differently now than they did before."

"Yes," John said. "They're expecting you to fit into a role they didn't see you in before."

I still wasn't sure what John meant. "I don't feel that I'm being insincere *about any of this," I said. "I'm not trying to act as if I'm better than I am to sat-isfy them. At least I don't think I am."*

"No," John explained. "But you're probably finding that you've had to grow into the role they have provided for you."

As I have thought about John's insight, I think he's right.

. . .

David's side wound continued to close up, and now it was shaped like England. But the skin was very slow in spreading, and so our Provo plastic surgeon suggested an operation to finish closing David's chest, side, elbow, and to put extra skin in his armpit and on his inner arm to allow more movement. Later David had another operation to try again to cover the elbow with skin. Elbows are very tricky. In every skin graft operation, the doctors "harvested" skin from his thighs, so he had painful thigh wounds to care for too. Then he had to wear an elastic nylon suit over his upper legs, trunk, and arm for over an entire year. The Jobst suit puts con-stant twenty-four-hour pressure on all the skin grafts and scars so that they will heal flat and smooth. *Jobst* is pronounced *Job's,* like the Biblical character—presumably, David often said, because one needs the patience of Job to wear it. Since the suit is made of nylon and rubber, it is extremely hot to wear, especially in the summer. David hated it. We jokingly call the suit his steel-belted support hose.

By this time we began to receive the bills from all the doctors and hospitals. This became overwhelming for me to deal with, so I finally set up a manila folder for each doctor, hospital, ambulance service, and lab. By the end, the insurance forms and doctors' bills took up a good eight inches in my file cabi-net. I spent hours and hours on the telephone with doctors' billing services and the insurance company trying to straighten everything out. In the end, our insurance changed its policy of always charging us 2 percent, and it paid most everything after four thousand dollars. Because the hospital discounted the bill for the insurance company, we did not go over the million-dollar limit, so we still have insurance and are not bankrupt.

We received more than just bills in the mail. Many of our friends wrote us letters and cards and faxes over the months of David's illness. I organized all these letters, and more pleasantly, the size of the letter files is twice the size of the bills files.

David spent a year on disability, during which he worked full-time on recovering. He lifted weights, went to painful physical therapy sessions, spent a lot of time putting lotion and sunscreen on his skin grafts, and went walking with me to build up his cardiovascular system. He also used homeopathy to help himself recover completely from thirteen operations and the total exhaustion of the experience.

During his recovery he developed a little bit of a poochy stomach. This really bothered him, so he tried to lose weight. Very quickly he discovered this was the wrong thing to do because he lost all of his energy, so he kept the little pooch (we call it Poochito). I figured that because of the fat layers he lost all over his body, he developed a little extra around his stomach just to keep his body going.

David worked hard to get the range of motion back into his arm. After many painful therapy sessions, he was able to move it and bend it just like before his sickness. His friend, former tennis companion, and fellow Victorian literature specialist, Steve, called David up one day.

"How about going out and hitting a few tennis balls," Steve asked.

"Yes, I think I am ready," was David's excited reply.

"Just don't try to serve and don't overdo it," I warned as he left, although I knew he would try to serve and he certainly would overdo it.

Within a month David was playing doubles regularly and singles occasionally. The many friends who jokingly challenged him to play tennis before he had fully recovered soon found his old game was returning.

And much to his son's delight, David could once again throw football passes as Steven ran complex patterns and made spectacular catches in the front yard.

Silver Lake

I had missed many things during my long rehabilitation: playing tennis, teaching and working with students, writing my novel. Among the things I most looked forward to were camping and hiking again.

I had long enjoyed camping, occasionally throwing a foam pad, a sleeping bag, and a camp stove in the back of the minivan and driving off to some solitary place to work on my novel. I explored locations important to my novel. Other times I parked by a secluded beach where, sheltered from the wind by the van, I plugged my notebook computer into the cigarette lighter and wrote for hours, looking out occasionally at the sun reflecting off the ocean water or watching for migrating whales swimming by.

By mid-August 1995, I felt well enough that we counted our money, purchased a tent, and decided to spend the weekend camping. We cautiously chose a campground close to home in case my optimism exceeded my strength. Thursday, August 10, Delys and Robby drove me to a beautiful campground in a nearby mountain canyon. We arrived in time to get the last unoccupied site. The heavy winter snowfall had created a stream that ran past our campsite. No one could remember ever having seen one there before. I nearly cried to find myself engulfed in the shade of pines and aspens and the smells and sounds of the woods.

Someone had to stay the night to keep the campsite, and I eventually overcame Delys's misgivings and talked her into letting me spend Thursday night alone. Delys had to teach the next day, the children had their own commitments, and besides, I wanted to prove to myself that I could survive the night on my own. As Delys and Robby drove away, I felt a sense of exhilaration and freedom that reminded me of my feelings when I had escaped from the hospital almost exactly six months before.

Friday afternoon Delys returned with our three youngest children. Cristie and Kathryn stayed in Provo to work and party.

We spent Friday and Saturday rather restfully together. Sunday, August 13, was Delys's and my nineteenth wedding anniversary. We agreed to postpone our traditional night out until a few days later. During the morning we met around the picnic table for a short family worship service. Then we broke camp, loaded up the minivan, and drove off to explore parts of the local canyons we had not seen before.

After several hours of driving, we stopped for lunch at a place high in the mountains called Silver Lake Flats. We fixed sandwiches next to a beautiful reservoir. After lunch, I noticed a sign that read "Silver Lake Trail 1½ miles."

"Let's walk up a little way," I said. I didn't dare suggest what I really thought: that though a three-mile round-trip was farther than I had ever gone since my illness, I might actually be able to make it. The trail seemed level and pleasantly shaded. My spirit nearly shouted aloud for me to do the impossible.

"Yea," screamed all the kids. I think they felt anything was better than getting back into the hot car and driving again.

I sneaked a look at Delys to see if she knew what I was really thinking. If she did, she didn't show it, though I have learned that she usually knows exactly what's on my mind regardless of what I say.

"All right," Delys said. "We can go until you start getting tired. Then we'll rest and come back."

As we began walking slowly through the pines and aspens, I felt a powerful sense of exhilaration. Rob kept getting ahead in his thirteen-year-old enthusiasm. I tried to stay as close behind him as I could, though my pace was slower. Periodically we stopped while Delys, Marissa, and Steven caught up.

At one point, while we were waiting for Steven and Marissa to rest, Steven complained of being tired.

"You don't have to go all the way if you don't want to," I told him, talking to myself, perhaps, even more than to Steven. "You can decide that for yourself, and there's no shame in not wanting to do something. But I've always felt that if you do actually decide to accomplish something, you have to do whatever it takes." I recognized that that sounded a bit stupid, probably another case of latent machismo. But I have always tried to act that way. That was part of what helped me get through a rigorous Ph.D. program. And it was certainly crucial to my continuing recovery.

I also knew that I was going to get to the end of the Silver Lake Trail and back, no matter what it took.

As we rounded the next bend, we discovered the trail suddenly steepened considerably. *This is going to be harder than I thought,* I realized. But I was still determined.

Soon the trail rose at a horrific angle. We had to climb using our hands as much as our feet over large, slippery, loose rocks that constituted the alleged "trail." I was beginning to think I had set myself up for failure this time.

We stopped to rest frequently. At one point we could see a ridge high above us.

"That must be it," Delys said. "I think we should turn back now. You'll never get all the way up there."

"Well, let's at least go a little farther," I said. I wasn't beaten yet, though I, too, doubted my ability to climb that high. I hadn't realized that "1½ miles" apparently referred to the increase in elevation as well as the length of the trail.

After what seemed like forever, we finally reached the elusive ridge. I looked around expectantly for the lake, but it wasn't there. Rob, who had arrived first as usual, was grinning and pointing upward. "It must be the next ridge," he said, starting off with more bounce in his walk than I could forgive.

"You stay here," Delys ordered. There was no brooking that command. "We'll go on and let you know how much farther it is." She could see, as I could feel, that I was on the verge of collapse.

A few minutes later I heard Delys calling back down to me. "Stay put," she said. "It's even worse than before. Wait where you are. We're going to the top, and then we'll come right back down."

I knew she was right. I wasn't at all certain I could get back down the mountain from where I was now, let alone continue climbing. I waited impatiently for a few minutes while some of my strength returned. I looked up at the high ridge above me. I shook my head at my own lunacy as I found myself slowly climbing again.

The last quarter mile was the worst. I wasn't sure I could continue from one step to the next, and I had to stop to rest every few yards, but I wouldn't quit this close to the top. Rob the Eternally Energetic had come back to check on me. He encouraged me, telling me it wasn't much farther until the ground leveled out again.

On top of the ridge the trail became nearly level. I thought, *I've made it!* But my legs still threatened to buckle at every step. I literally staggered.

Rounding the last bend, I suddenly saw a vision of mountain beauty, intensified by what it had taken to get there. A beautiful lake sparkled in the sun, surrounded by cliffs of green-dotted basalt. We counted five thin waterfalls trickling down the cliffs. In the water fish jumped.

"That's how fish commit suicide," said Rob. "It's like a person jumping off a bridge into the water."

Jumping into the water sounded great to me right then, though the still-open patches where my skin grafts had not yet taken precluded that. There are limits even to my insanity.

We sat peacefully for half an hour or so, until the sinking sun reminded us that we still had a long hike ahead. I knew my own energy levels were pretty thoroughly depleted, and we had drunk most of our water on the way up. Rob volunteered to run back to the car and return with supplies while the rest of us descended at a more reasonable pace. We gave him a head start, then began slowly walking back.

Though not as difficult as the climb up had been, the trip down involved different muscles as we attempted to negotiate the loose rocks without slipping and falling down the steep trail.

Before long we saw Rob, actually running, carrying boxes of fruit juice and granola bars. As we stopped to refresh ourselves, I realized that if he hadn't come, I might not have made it back.

We finally reached the car just before the sun set behind the mountain we had climbed. I knew I had just done something crazy. (In fact, when I told my therapist, Ron Nuttall, about it the next day, he said that one reason for my speedy recovery was the stupid things I kept doing.) But I felt almost giddy at having made the impossible hike.

As we drove back toward our home, I realized that this climb somehow encapsulated my whole experience of the previous eight months. The Silver Lake climb was a tremendous struggle to do something I would not have believed possible if I hadn't actually done it. The success came only after much pain and difficulty, and it came at a price. It required every ounce of determination I could muster. It was something I could only get through with valiant help from others, especially my family. It involved significant personal growth, both physical and spiritual. And it was something I would never have chosen to do had I known what it involved, though afterward I would not have traded the experience for anything.

Tennis with Dr. Shin

Even though everyone thought we were crazy, we decided to try California for Christmas again the next year. This time I zipped up all the packed suitcases myself. David decided to call Dr. Shin ahead of time. He eventually found the number and called to remind him of the tennis challenge David made in the hospital when Dr. Shin predicted he would never be able to play again. It took Dr. Shin a minute to figure out who David was. When he finally did, he was overjoyed, and surprised David could even hold a racquet. They agreed to play over the holidays.

On our way to California, we rehearsed what had happened just a year ago. My daughters Cristie and Kathryn and I made sure we did not stop at the same gas station or eating places in Las Vegas. Even though we knew intellectually that the strep A bacteria are all around us, and though we don't know exactly when David became infected, we were still wary of that gas station bathroom.

We spent the whole vacation remembering what we were doing on that day a year before. Early in the morning of December 24—exactly one year from the date the symptoms began—David and I drove to a community park where we met Dr. Shin. We talked with him on the tennis courts for a while and met Dr. Shin's tennis partners. Dr. Shin had called the local newspaper, so after a bit, the photographer and reporter showed up for interviews and pictures. Dr. Shin and David played doubles as partners, and they won the set with the incredible score of 6–0. After that they split up and split two more sets. Every time David hit an ace or a particularly nice shot, even against him, Dr. Shin laughed with glee. He kept calling David over to the net to look at the grafts and to shake his head in near disbelief over the muscle tone and ability to use his right arm. David kept having to lift his shirt so Dr. Shin could point things out to one of the other players, who was also a physician. Three sets are a lot for middle-aged men, especially for someone who hasn't quite recovered from a ravaging disease.

The newspaper story appeared as the lead front-page article, with a color picture of David hitting the tennis ball. While the rest of us admired the article, David was particularly pleased that the form on his forehand looked so good in the picture.

. . .

After the game, Dr. Shin stayed to talk with us for nearly an hour next to the net post. We learned things that made the miraculous nature of the whole experience even more apparent. For one thing, Dr. Shin's presence when the ambulance rushed me to the hospital Emergency Room was fortuitous, to say the least. As a surgeon, Dr. Shin said, he virtually never went there. But that day one of his patients had suffered an injury, and Dr. Shin had dropped in to check on him. When the Emergency Room personnel couldn't figure out what was wrong with me, they asked Dr. Shin if he would examine me and offer an opinion. He got the process started, ordered tests, and then left to take care of other duties.

While Dr. Shin was gone, other physicians completed the tests that convinced them I had necrotizing fasciitis. One doctor told Delys that he didn't normally do the kind of operation I needed, but that it was essential that I get to surgery immediately. There wasn't time to send for anyone else.

While he was scrubbing for the operation, Dr. Shin returned to check on me. The other physician explained what my condition was and said he planned to cut across my abdominal cavity to expose the disease's path. Dr. Shin told us he "felt strongly" for some reason that this was exactly the wrong thing to do. The two doctors debated the issue for a few minutes. Finally Dr. Shin pulled rank. Since he had been the first physician to see me, technically I was his patient. Dr. Shin said he would perform the operation, opening me vertically "from wrist to hip" instead of horizontally across the body cavity. He said he would welcome the other doctor's assistance, but that if he couldn't agree, he was free to leave and Dr. Shin would find someone else to assist. He left, and Dr. Shin operated.

Afterward, it was clear that Dr. Shin had been correct. Had the other physician opened my body cavity, the bacteria would almost certainly have spread into my exposed vital organs. I would have died within hours. As it was, the bacteria conveniently invaded my arm, both sides, my abdomen, and my back but amazingly missed all the crucial organs. Had Dr. Shin not been present just at the moment I arrived at the hospital, and had he not felt so strongly what he should do, I would almost certainly have died.

Dr. Shin also explained that during the first week of operations, the surgeons had to guess repeatedly in which directions the bacteria would spread and what to do to stop it. Dr. Shin said that each time he had to guess, he "felt" what the best solution might be. The surgeons gambled on these feelings again and again, and every time they found they had done precisely the right thing. We smiled and reminded Dr. Shin that we believed he was guided in answer to the many prayers offered on our behalf. Though not prone to find religious explanations in such things, Dr. Shin nodded and said, "I don't doubt it."

As Dr. Shin recalled his feelings during those first dark days and recounted what he had done to battle the disease, Delys and I found ourselves increasingly amazed at what had occurred and at the incredible odds against my being alive—let alone with my body substantially intact. Dr. Shin said he would have wagered heavily against the slightest possibility of my ever playing tennis again. But here we were on the tennis court happily remembering the horrors and triumphs of the experience as something past and over.

Dr. Shin is obviously a gifted surgeon as well as a caring and giving person. But even his abilities alone—and those of Dr. Britto, Dr. Saketkhoo, and the other medical personnel who worked long and hard to save my life—could not have succeeded without the guidance of a power beyond their own. We remembered the words of Dr. John, the pharmacist. "Don't thank me," he said repeatedly, pointing up. "Thank Him. Everything I did for you quite clearly came to me from someplace else. You've obviously got friends in high places."

. . .

A few days after the tennis game, on December 27, we decided to celebrate David's recovery by visiting the hospital. Coincidentally, this visit took place exactly one year from the day the ambulance had taken David to the hospital.

We walked into the physical therapy section and told the receptionist David Cowles was here. Several therapists heard his name, and they came running out to see the man they had spent so much time helping. We went back by the whirlpool and found out how everyone was doing. Rebecca had moved. Everyone else was there. Stephanie and Joyce could hardly believe how healthy David looked, and I realized that they had only known him as a very sick man. Stephanie later wrote us these words:

Today, December 27, 1995, was one of the great days of my life. David came to see me, healthy cheeks full of color and smiling, well and whole. Words can't really express the emotion! The tears that fell from all the people gathered at this small reunion tell the story. David is a miracle. God had his hand in every move that was made, every decision, I'm convinced of that.

David has battle scars—I saw them today. He wears them proudly because he is a survivor. To this day I cannot speak about David without great emotion and awe. Such a will to live—he could settle for nothing less.

We said good-bye to the physical therapists and then walked up to the Critical Care Units on the third floor. As we passed my favorite elbow trees, I looked down to check out the hummingbird nest. It was gone.

We went to the first room David was in. Many of the nurses and the respiratory therapists recognized us and came to talk with us, telling us that the hospital was abuzz with the news that David Cowles was there visiting. David was amazed at what the room looked like from the outside, because he had been on morphine and only semiconscious when he was there. We got to see Teri and other nurses, and they got to see what David looked like as a healthy man. Then David and I walked alone to his second room in Critical Care. No one was in it, and someone in the hall quipped that we should name it the David Cowles Memorial Room since our hospital bill probably had completely paid for it. David walked over to the window and looked down at the beautiful quad below.

"Funny, when I was here I didn't even know there was a garden down there. All I could see was the roof and a bit of sky."

Joyce, the physical therapist, wrote to David after our visit: "I thank God that I had the opportunity to be a part of your healing. Your courage and faith have been an inspiration. Your miracle has become ours. I can't tell you the joy your recent visit to Whittier brought to us. To see you standing there before us, smiling, well, whole again is the best gift anyone could ask for."

For us, too.

But there was also sad news. We learned that Dr. John, the hospital's pharmacist and part-time comic who had been so supportive of David, had suffered a heart attack himself and died a few months after David was released. This shook us up for a while. Here was a man who for months helped a very sick patient recover from a deadly bacteria, and he himself died shortly afterward. We mourn his loss.

The Personal Factor

As I write this last chapter, it has been a year and a half since that fateful Christmas Day in 1994 when my life changed profoundly and permanently. I still lack some of my previous endurance, both physical and mental. I can't pull all-nighters anymore, but then, who wants to? It's probably not an entirely bad thing to have to use a bit of wisdom about how hard I work and how much time I spend with other things, such as my family. Still, I do most of what I could do before, just not for quite as long.

I still play tennis regularly, and my few remaining physical limitations have forced me to raise my concentration level, which has probably improved my overall game. I find my mental toughness has increased tremendously. And I am unquestionably happier after losing than I used to be.

I play the piano every day, letting my emotions and spiritual yearnings flow out of my fingers, into the keys, through the air to my ears, where they reenter my spirit in therapeutic and uplifting ways. I continue to compose, and I am currently working toward producing a compact disc of my own material.

I have just finished teaching my first full-time load. That experience exhausted my depleted body and mind but thrilled my yearning spirit. I recognize now more than ever how much I love teaching students to understand powerful ideas and appreciate artistic beauty, and then helping them connect these priceless things with their lives in positive ways. Teaching ideally exemplifies the best kinds of love and service, and I aspire to teach in that way.

I find now, more than a year after the worst is over, that I have repressed the memories of much of my experience those first weeks. Every now and then something will occur, often at unexpected moments, that will bring the whole picture back with devastating clarity. A PBS program about Critical Care

Units, news of a friend's surgery, a television report about a burn victim—and suddenly I find myself engulfed in uncontrollable feelings of horror and fear. I don't remember these feelings most of the time. My conscious memory seems to have blocked out the worst of it. But at these moments the full emotional impact of my battles, the horror of my helplessness, my frustration and confusion, and a deep revulsion at the memory of it all overpowers me. This has happened enough times now that I can only assume the experience must have been even worse—much worse—than I can consciously face. Writing this book has been both therapeutic and, at times, emotionally difficult.

Despite all the hardships, however, my illness has been one of the most profoundly valuable experiences of my entire life. It has made me a different person—a better person in many ways. It would be impossible to compute everything I have learned and every way my experience has made me better, or at least different. Much of what I have learned defies the merciless limits of language. But some things clearly stand out to me, even from the relatively short perspective of a few months.

For one thing, I have found that my spirit is much more sensitive, both to good and to bad things around me. I found that certain language and attitudes offend me much more than they did before. I am more selective about what books I read and what videos I watch. Things just bother me more, and I have lost interest in things that once might have intrigued me. Especially in the first months after my return home, I found my spiritual sensitivity greatly heightened.

On the other hand, I have also found myself more patient and tolerant of other people who don't see things the same way I do. My own increased spiritual sensitivity, hopefully, does not translate into harsher judgments of others. Knowing how far from godlike I have been, and continue to be, and how wrong I have been about many things in my own life, I am obviously in no position to question someone else's beliefs or judge them when they disagree with me.

I have also learned that one can accomplish almost anything with hard work, determination, the support of others, and spiritual conviction. However, I also learned that some things are much more worthy of that kind of effort than others.

After nearly dying, I kept asking myself what my life would have meant had it ended suddenly just after Christmas 1994. I found that my priorities needed some adjusting. Things that had seemed essential before suddenly appeared inconsequential, and many things I had not given much attention to seemed crucial now.

152

For starters, material things meant nearly nothing. Cars, clothes, computers, stereo equipment, even my cherished grand piano—all had lost most of the luster they once possessed. They weren't worth even considering in a more eternal view of life and its meaning.

I found, too, that the importance of what had seemed the great issues of the day—political, religious, ideological—had dimmed considerably. Our petty differences—the ones that keep us arguing, that make brothers and sisters into enemies—seemed only to get in the way of the love and caring that really mattered. Far from being crucial determiners of a person's worth, they appeared to me now largely as hindrances to more important matters.

Even things that I had spent much of my time doing—valuable things that I am still proud of—seemed less important than before. My academic degrees and accomplishments, my publications, the awards I had received, even the positions I had held in my church, all seemed to matter less than I might have thought. I still spend much time and effort in these areas, and I think the work I do is good and useful. But I now see these things more as means than I once did, less as ends in themselves. The projects I work on now—such as this book—must show clear ethical and even spiritual value to be worth my time.

On the other hand, I was surprised at some of the things that really did come to matter to me. I knew my family was important, but I had somehow never sensed how much each of them meant. I spent literally hours in my hospital bed staring at the family portrait Delys had left for me. I missed each of my children individually and my entire family collectively. I could hardly bear to think that I had too often chosen to do other things when I might have been spending time with them.

Surprisingly, among the things that mattered most were the small, easily forgotten acts of kindness I had sometimes managed to commit—the too-rare times I had helped someone, often with nothing more than a kind word or a smile. I found I valued the times I had encouraged students, family members, friends, and colleagues, the occasional times I had secretly performed some act of generosity or service.

I also found I valued the moments of real spiritual contact—with God and with other people. These were the moments when I experienced real growth and real love. I work much harder now to make those moments occur more frequently and more intensely. What really matters, when all is said and done, is the human soul—our own, and those of others. What makes the soul stronger, more *spiritual, more complete, more loving, more like God—that matters; everything else is important only as it makes the growth of our souls easier.*

One of my great disappointments has been the recognition of how often the pressures and trivialities of life keep pulling me down from the spiritual mountain-top on which my illness left me. Still, I believe that only in this constant battle with the mundane can true spirituality really develop and shine. Like John Milton, I cannot much respect "a fugitive and a cloistered virtue."

. . .

Unfortunately, we have not turned into perfect people. I still occasionally offend others when I do not intend to, and I never sat down and wrote those three hundred thank-you notes to the many people who helped us. David's temper rises in traffic and sometimes in the confusion of living with five children, their friends, and the resultant clutter. We have teenagers who can be moody and younger children who can be loud. And even though all seven of us play musical instruments, none of us likes to hear anyone else practicing.

Even so, each of us has been greatly affected by David's illness and recovery. We know that God knows who we are, and we know he has blessed us in obvious ways. In our case, God has blessed the meek of the earth, not just the mighty. People often ask me how I was able to handle everything terrible that was happening to our family at that time. I reply that those many prayers were not just for David but also for the rest of our family so that we could be spiritually sustained. The prayers brought me peace.

We have been pleased to share David's miracle with other people who consider it their miracle too, for God has blessed many by allowing David to recover. Together we can create miracles, and in doing so we bring communities together. We have been buoyed up by all the service our congregation performed for our family, everything from faxing notes of encouragement to moving furniture to welcoming David home to feeding us. We have been very blessed to live in a caring neighborhood.

My brother Brent and sister, Wendy, started a charitable fund for David, and this money made it possible for me to fly back and forth to Los Angeles and helped pay for the hundreds of medical bills. In the end we are not bankrupt as I once thought we would be. We have been physically sustained.

Before this illness, David could easily become emotionally down. He would complain and become upset if something undeserved happened to him. During the illness, though, his attitude was amazing. He rarely com-plained, he never moaned "Why did this happen to me," and he was very patient and positive. As one of the physical therapists said, "I am sure that much of David's calmness came from his medications, but just the same, it would be the calmness, the courage I would see each time I worked with him over the next several weeks." Obviously, he was emotionally sus-tained through God's grace.

Our family was emotionally sustained, too. We had a lot we could have complained about, but we saw so much good that our complaints seemed trivial. When school let out that year, David was feeling much stronger, so Mom and Dad Cowles flew us out to Portland to visit them. There we got to hear about how kind, concerned, and prayerful the Portland church members were during David's illness. We got to visit family and relax in the forests. When we flew back home to the Salt Lake City airport, I told my family to wait at the baggage section while I fetched the car from the long-term parking lot. As I exited the shuttle bus and walked over to the car, I noticed one of the tires had gone completely flat. I knew there was a slow leak in that tire, so I went inside the car to find the Fix-a-flat. On the other side of the car, I was surprised to find two more tires flat. Three flat tires. I could hardly believe it. Eventually the airport repair service helped me pump up the tires, since they all seemed to have slow leaks, and I drove to baggage claim an hour late to pick up my concerned family.

A few days later I was telling a friend about our airport experience. I told her I came to the car and found three flat tires. Can you believe that? Then I said, "Wait, after all that has happened to our family this past year, I really must restate that. I came to the car and found one fully inflated tire!"

My family has laughed over this line many times since. We have been emotionally sustained because we were able to focus on the great blessings in our life like that one fully inflated tire.

And I find my prayers have mostly become prayers of thanks. The line from the hymn often echoes in my thoughts: "Oh, what shall I ask of thy providence more?"

. . .

My in-laws were reading through my father-in-law's meticulous journal for 1990 as they traveled to Provo a few months ago. My father-in-law had recorded a comment I had made in a church lesson he had taught that year about prayer. I apparently said (with uncharacteristic wisdom) that we should not pray that nothing bad will happen to us, but that we will have the kind of attitude that will turn whatever does happen into a blessing.

One of the most frequent responses to my story is, "I'm sure you must have agonized over why this should happen to you." Or in another common variant, "You must really wonder why God would do this to you."

In truth, this isn't the question I found myself asking. Perhaps this was because from my first conscious moments everyone kept telling me what a miracle my survival was. In addition, I immediately remembered the blessing my father-in-law had given me when we all thought I had a simple case of stomach flu. My mind echoed with the inspired assurance that "the illness that is eating at your body" would be cured, and that the whole experience was intended to teach me many things, including empathy for the sufferings of others.

These perspectives helped me view my illness and recovery in a much more positive light. Instead of asking "Why me?" about contracting this horrible disease, I found myself asking "Why should God have blessed me with this miracle? Why should he care about me enough to teach me what I must learn from all this?" That doesn't mean I was always happy about my suffering. But under the circumstances, excessive complaining seems utterly absurd.

It appears to me now, after having been through the worst of the experience, that most of life's problems are really potential blessings. My favorite poet, Robert Browning, puts it this way:

Is this our ultimate stage, or starting-place
To try man's foot, if it will creep or climb,
'Mid obstacles in seeming, points that prove
Advantage for who vaults from low to high
And makes the stumbling-block a stepping-stone?
(*The Ring and the Book,* book 10, lines 408–12)

I can't take any particular credit for whatever I have managed to do well through this experience. For one thing, the help and support of family, friends, and many others made my part much easier than it might have been. Their sustaining love and prayers have had a profound effect on me throughout my illness and recovery.

I also credit those prayers for the clear sense I felt from the beginning that God's hand was in this, and that he was sustaining and strengthening me far beyond my own capacities. I am convinced that many of the best things in our lives—our love for others, our sense of God's love for us, our ability to deal with pain, loss, and frustration—come to us not by an act of will but by an act of grace. This has certainly been so in my case.

As I try to sum up my life and feelings since I first woke up in the hospital, I feel an overwhelming sense of love and peace. Obviously I have lost some things: time, comfort, endurance, certain physical capacities. But I have gained so much more that I can only identify this as the most profound and important single experience of my life, and be grateful for what it has taught me.

Ultimately, though you could never pay me enough to go through this experience again, I wouldn't trade it for anything—not to have my healthy body back, not to have avoided all the pain and anguish, not for everything I lost and much more.

The words of Paul to the Corinthians have come to mean more to me than ever before:

> And he said unto me, My grace is sufficient for thee: for my strength is made perfect in weakness. Most gladly therefore will I rather glory in my infirmities, that the power of Christ may rest upon me. Therefore I take pleasure in infirmities, in reproaches, in necessities, in persecutions, in distresses for Christ's sake: for when I am weak, then am I strong. (2 Corinthians 12:9–10.)

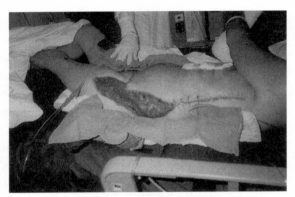

David's left side mostly stitched up, but some left for future skin grafts to cover.

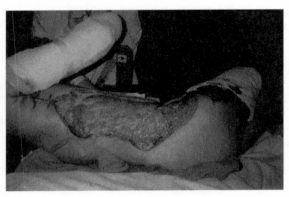

David's right side, stitched from the armpit to upper chest. The rest would be covered by skin grafts.

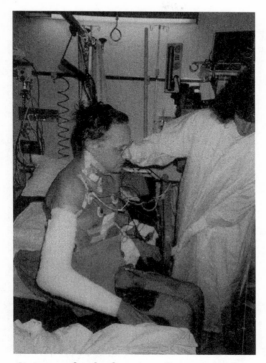

Sitting up for the first time. Scars on his legs
show where skin was taken for grafts.

David today, recovered to an active life of
teaching, sports, and outdoor activity.